With Best Wishes

עם ברכה

Alec Shmuely

Adaia Shumuely

9/98

A Bridge Across the Jordan

A Bridge Across the Jordan

*The Friendship Between
a Jewish Carpenter and
the King of Jordan*

Adaia and Abraham Shumsky

ARCADE PUBLISHING • NEW YORK

FIRST EDITION

Library of Congress Cataloging-in Publication Data

Shumsky, Adaia.
    A bridge across the Jordan : the friendship between a Jewish carpenter and the King of Jordan / by Adaia and Abraham Shumsky.
—1st ed.
        p.   cm.
    ISBN 1-55970-391-1
    1. Cohen, Mendel, 1895–1970—Friends and associates.   2. Israelis—Biography.   3. Abdullah, King of Jordan, 1882–1951—Friends and associates. 4. Jordan—Kings and rulers—Biography.   I. Shumsky, Abraham, 1921– . II. Title.
CT1919.P38C677 1977
956.9504'092—dc21   97–12871

Published in the United States by Arcade Publishing, Inc., New York
Distributed by Little, Brown and Company

10 9 8 7 6 5 4 3 2 1

PRINTED IN THE UNITED STATES OF AMERICA

To the memory of

Tova and Mendel Cohen

Contents

Part II
From Amman, 1995

ACKNOWLEDGMENTS

MY FATHER'S EXPERIENCES at the court of King Abdullah of Jordan were an adventure that would not have happened had it not been for my mother's endurance and support. I often think of my parents as a rock and a balloon attached to each other by a string. My mother was the rock — solid, predictable, embedded in the soil, too modest to attract notice. My father was the balloon — colorful, exciting, ready to embark on the next flight. Without the string, the balloon would have vanished into the air, and the rock would have led a drab existence. I want to thank my parents for enriching my life with rock gardens and balloon flights.

Thanks also to my brother Ardon Cohen, who was partner to the joys and sorrows surrounding my father's travels between Jerusalem and Amman. Ardon was instrumental in organizing a family trip to Raghdan Palace in 1995, and helped this project proceed by sharing his bottomless fund of information and family reminiscences with us. And to the members of the family — children, grandchildren, and great-grandchildren of Tova and Mendel — who traveled with us to Jordan, our thanks for bringing the family closer together.

Our daughter Alina and her husband David, and our son Ron and his wife Naho, assisted with useful reactions, reviewing the manuscript periodically, offering detailed suggestions, and encouraging us when the going got rough. To them, their children, and their future grandchildren, here is a family story they may wish one day to explore on their own.

Friends kept our spirits up and our minds alert through their interest in our progress and their helpful feedback. Among them were Eleanor Adiel, Ruth Goldman and Art McDonnell, Dr. Bernard and Barbara Leibman, Barbara November, and Dr. Margaret Waters. Special thanks to our friends Hanoch Bartov and Sandra Rosencrans, who offered new perspectives on the project and who reminded us that "God is in the details."

Our sincere gratitude to Timothy Bent at Arcade Publishing for his belief in the message of the book and his assiduous work on the manuscript. Always constructive in his recommendations and mindful of our intent, he gave us invaluable support. We also wish to thank Ann Marlowe for her erudite and careful copyediting.

Last but foremost, our thanks to His Majesty King Hussein, who invited us to Amman and in his generosity made the necessary arrangements for our visit to the palace. Most helpful were Professor Mohammad Bakhit, president of Al al-Bayt University in Jordan, who provided us with valuable information about King Abdullah and his time, and King Hussein's staff, who guided us throughout the visit.

The authors, a husband-and-wife team, have based this book on the diaries of Mendel Cohen and on their own recent visit to Jordan and to the royal palace in Amman. The retelling of Mendel Cohen's experiences in Amman is narrated in his voice. The account of the authors' visit is narrated in the voice of his daughter, Adaia Shumsky.

Titles have changed during the period covered in the book. In 1946 Abdullah's title changed from "emir" to "king" and the name of his country from Transjordan to the Hashemite Kingdom of Jordan. The areas west of the Jordan, called Palestine before 1947, are referred to at the time of this writing as Israel and the West Bank.

When friends ask, "How is it to write a book together?" we reply, "Not easy! Don't try it unless your marriage is rock-solid and has lasted many years!" We feel enriched by the experience, and by our differences and their resolution, as we reach the fiftieth year of our partnership.

Adaia and Abraham Shumsky
Great Neck, New York, 1997

THE HASHEMITE ROYAL DYNASTY

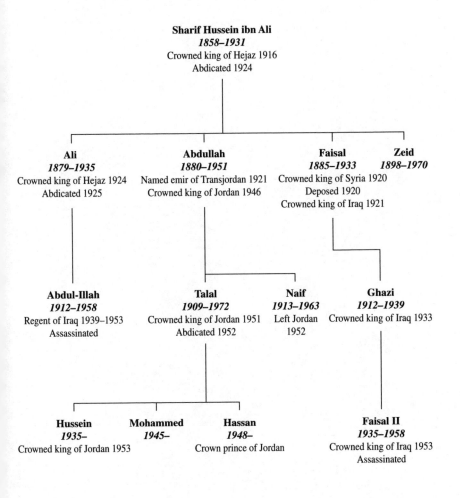

Sharif Hussein ibn Ali
1858–1931
Crowned king of Hejaz 1916
Abdicated 1924

Ali
1879–1935
Crowned king of Hejaz 1924
Abdicated 1925

Abdullah
1880–1951
Named emir of Transjordan 1921
Crowned king of Jordan 1946

Faisal
1885–1933
Crowned king of Syria 1920
Deposed 1920
Crowned king of Iraq 1921

Zeid
1898–1970

Abdul-Illah
1912–1958
Regent of Iraq 1939–1953
Assassinated

Talal
1909–1972
Crowned king of Jordan 1951
Abdicated 1952

Naif
1913–1963
Left Jordan
1952

Ghazi
1912–1939
Crowned king of Iraq 1933

Hussein
1935–
Crowned king of Jordan 1953

Mohammed
1945–

Hassan
1948–
Crown prince of Jordan

Faisal II
1935–1958
Crowned king of Iraq 1953
Assassinated

INTRODUCTION

My Father's King

THE TRIP FROM JERUSALEM TO AMMAN is a mere two-hour car ride, but marked by inordinate extremes. The cool mountain air of Jerusalem, with its fragrant odors of cypress and pine, gives way to the dry, oppressive heat generated by a relentless sun hitting the Judean desert. The road gradually descends, past gaunt black goats grazing on the meager stalks of yellowing grass, to the oasis of Jericho, nestled deep in the rift of the Jordan Valley — then, as the road ascends, the air begins to cool again, villages appear along the road, and Amman emerges, perched like her older sister Jerusalem on a group of hills.

This is the road my father traveled frequently, pursuing a most unusual venture. Half a century later, I am retracing my father's steps by retelling the bittersweet story of my father's king.

The story begins sixty years ago when my father, Mendel Cohen, went to work at the court of then-Emir Abdullah of Jordan, grandfather of the present monarch, King Hussein. What is most unusual is that the emir/king and my father, his employee, became friends. One was an Arab, the other a Jew, one was born in the holy city of Mecca to a family of great distinction, the other in the holy city of Jerusalem to a humble carpenter. They held incompatible political aspirations and followed different faiths, but they formed a friendship that transcended their differences and the hostilities that surrounded them.

My father worked as a carpenter for Abdullah from 1937 until the outbreak of the war between Israel and the Arabs in 1948. He recorded the story of his experiences at the Jordanian royal court in the form of a memoir. When I decided to retell his story, I wrote to King Hussein, asking for permission to visit the court at Amman, where the events described in the memoirs had taken place. King Hussein's response arrived in just two weeks:

November 25, 1994

Dear Friend,

Thank you very much indeed for your kind message of congratulations and interesting letter of November 6th, 1994. It was very thoughtful of you to write and tell me about the good friendship that existed between my late grandfather and your late father. It would give me great pleasure to give you permission to visit the Royal Court in March or April, 1995, so that you can complete your late father's English version of his diary. Please liaise with the Director of my Private Office, Colonel Ali Shukri, so that all the necessary arrangements can be made.

I am
Your sincere friend,
Hussein

I first heard of Abdullah one blustery February midday. Huddled around a kerosene heater, we were waiting for my father in our home in Jerusalem. My father arrived in his usual hurried manner. He was working at the palace of the high commissioner of Palestine, and under pressure to get a project completed on time. Unlike most working men, who customarily returned to their homes for lunch and took a siesta of an hour or two, my father was always in a rush to meet the next deadline. This time, however, he did not run out. He had something funny to tell us, he said. While working at the palace he had been introduced to the emir of Transjordan, who expressed interest in commissioning him for a construction project. My father told us this almost casually, but my mother, with her keen senses, suspected that more might be at stake. She looked at him quizzically, wondering what the next surprise might be. She didn't have to wait long.

Soon after, my father embarked on a ten-year adventure as the chief builder and contractor to Emir Abdullah. Those were tumultuous years for the Jewish community in Palestine, and a time of great anxiety for the family. Tensions between Arabs and Jews had been escalating. Hajj Amin el-Husseini, the grand mufti of Jerusalem and the leader of the Arabs in Palestine, was waging a venomous campaign against Jewish immigration, spurring the Arab population to acts of violence, and spreading anti-Jewish propaganda to neighboring Arab countries. We feared for my father's life. We knew that the mufti and his sympathizers had no tolerance for Arabs employing Jews, particularly when the employer was an Arab leader of such eminence as Emir Abdullah.

Trying to allay our fears, my father, the consummate optimist, told us the emir and the mufti were archenemies and worlds apart in their attitude toward Jews. Unlike the mufti, Abdullah was seeking friendship and accommodation rather than confrontation and bloodshed. A Jew in Amman, he insisted, was probably safer than a Jew in Jerusalem.

We tried to be convinced, but when the time came for my father to leave it was difficult to stay calm, particularly at the sight of the armored car that transported him and his crew to Amman. My father explained that these precautions were needed only until the passage of the border, and that once he arrived in Transjordan he would be fine. This hardly eased our worry. We used to sit by the phone for hours, waiting for word of his safe arrival.

I remember feeling anxious about my father's trips to Amman, but I don't remember questioning his decision to go. His work came first. Work was a passion for him, akin to a religion; it was his cure-all, an answer to ailment, depression, boredom, aging, and other misfortunes. His work was also a part of our lives. He used to take us to see his projects — the belfry of the YMCA tower in Jerusalem; the Rivoli gift shop that was lined with mahogany shelves and cases for displaying jewelry, silver, and rare glass; the May Brothers' store, the first to import women's fashions from Europe; the carved ceiling of the King David Hotel; an Arab café in the Old City; a new pulpit at one of Jerusalem's ancient churches. He was always ready with a story about his latest project and the people with whom it brought him into contact. Listening to his stories made his projects ours too.

I often wonder how my mother managed during his frequent absences. She said little and was reluctant about showing her feelings. But I remember that she looked as if a burden had been lifted from her shoulders when he came home.

I didn't resent my father's absences, perhaps because I felt his support even when he wasn't there. I remember once when I was a high school student a competition in medieval Jewish history was announced. The winner was to be awarded a scholarship worth half a year's tuition. The field was not of particular interest to me, but I decided to enter anyway. The deeper I got into the subject, the more interested I became and the harder I worked. I won first prize.

One day I saw my father walking out of the principal's office.

"What are you doing here?" I asked, feeling alarmed. I knew he was home for a short visit and had lots of things to attend to.

"They called me in to congratulate me for your winning the competition," he replied with a smile. Then he added, "The truth is, they asked me to forgo the prize so that it could be awarded to a more needy student." He must have seen the anger building up in me. "Don't worry," he said, "I told them I was not the one who received it and it wasn't mine to give back."

No more was said, but I later found out that my father had repaid the school by equipping a whole classroom with desks.

My father compensated for his absence by filling our lives with his stories — mostly about the emir, whose world was only two hours away and yet so different and so mysterious. We listened breathlessly while he talked of desert caravans, warring tribes, villains, princes, and sheikhs. At the center of them all was the romantic figure of the Bedouin monarch himself, ruler over a desert land, with his silk robes and sword, astride his horses and camels. We felt very blessed; we knew of no other family with a king of its own.

One day my father returned home with a truly spectacular gift. It was a set of silver, numbering more than a hundred pieces, a gift from Abdullah. With the gift came another story. Upon the completion of his new dining room in the royal palace, Abdullah asked my father to return to Jerusalem and fetch him the most beautiful set of silver he could find. Cost was no object, he said, but the purchase had to be unique. This was a difficult assignment to carry out, for it was during the Second World War, when such luxuries were in short supply. However, my father discovered that among the Jewish refugees who had fled from Germany were a few who had managed to salvage some of their valuables and who were eager to exchange them for cash. He found the set he was looking for. The silver was classical in design, but each piece had a crescent engraved on it, fortuitously resembling the crescent and star symbol of Islam. When my father returned to Amman with the precious silver, Abdullah presented it to him in gratitude for the work he had done on his dining room.

The silverware adorned our family table every Sabbath and holiday. My father had a special felt-lined cabinet built to store it, and my mother kept it polished at all times. When my mother died, my father passed the silver on to me and I took it with me when I went to study in America. One rainy Sunday in 1973, my house was burglarized and the silver was stolen, never to be recovered.

During the Second World War relations between Arabs and Jews in Palestine improved. The British administration cracked down severely on internal turmoil within its territories, to create a unified front in the war against Germany. The grand mufti of Jerusalem, the chief instigator of the unrest, was exiled, and relative peace followed. The Jewish community in Palestine and the Hashemites of Transjordan closed ranks in their support of the British, while other Arab countries were tending toward supporting the Nazis. It was during that period that my father made many friends at the Jordanian court and in the city of Amman. Some of his friends visited our home in Jerusalem and extended their friendship to other members of the family.

First came Mohammed Zubati, an intimate of the king's, bringing nylon stockings, woolen tweeds, and exotic dried fruit, all items of great scarcity during wartime. Passersby would stop to watch the unusual sight of a tall Bedouin and his entourage stepping out of a large shiny black car. In his silk robe of white, black, and gold stripes, white headcloth fastened by a golden band, and gleaming dagger dangling down at his waist, Zubati looked like a figure out of an Arabian storybook.

Nahada, the emir's third wife, was also a frequent visitor in our home. When we heard the monarch's wife was coming, we expected the Queen of Sheba, wearing exotic Egyptian jewels and robes, but Nahada was dressed in Western suits and hats. She nevertheless radiated regal elegance in her movements and cascading laughter. Nahada and my mother chatted in Arabic and seemed to get along quite well.

Then there was Naif, the emir's second son, who acted most informally and who was always telling jokes I could not understand. My father used to say that Naif had inherited his father's love for joking but not his father's wit.

Preparation for these visitors was always a cause of frenzied commotion in our household as my mother attempted to make Arab dishes, a cuisine with which she was completely unfamiliar. The menu usually consisted of roasted lamb, rice with pine nuts and dried fruit, stuffed grape leaves, almond cakes, and an orchid-flavored pudding. Leftovers, which we normally preserved, were thrown away, because no one in the family developed a taste for lamb. The odor of the meat lingered in the house for days. I used to feel anxious about the visits of royalty to our house, thinking that the king and his family were accustomed to luxury and grandeur and would sneer at our humble home. These differences seemed of little consequence, though, and the visits were always filled with laughter and goodwill.

The wartime thaw between Arabs and Jews made it safe not only for the emir's inner circle to travel freely to Palestine but for us to visit Transjordan. Being the oldest child, I was given the option to take the first trip. As expected, my mother had reservations concerning the safety of such a venture, but my father insisted that it was absolutely safe. And, as usual, my mother's fears were overwhelmed by my father's confidence. She also gave in because, despite her objections, she shared a bit of his adventurous spirit and wanted her children to experience some of the same. So it was agreed that after my fourteenth birthday I would go to Amman. I felt privileged, believing that I was the first Jewish child to visit the Hashemite royal court.

We drove there by way of Jericho in a large car provided by the emir. When we passed the Allenby Bridge the border sentries stood at attention and saluted. As we were climbing out of the deep valley toward Amman, I saw from a distance a city perched on the hills. Stone houses were built along the slopes, their doors and windows painted turquoise (to ward off bad luck). We entered Amman through the narrow alleys of the soukh. Fruits and vegetables, brass and copper utensils, cloaks and scarves, blankets and rugs were all chaotically displayed in a medley of color and sound. Our driver tried to steer his way among the donkey and camel riders, honking his horn, which only had the effect of causing the donkeys to freeze in place and the camels to panic and run into the boxes and baskets of fruit on display.

Among shouts and friendly salutations we managed to get to the center of the city, the site of the ancient Roman theater, the Diwan or government headquarters, and the Philadelphia Hotel. "Philadelphia" in the middle of a Hashemite kingdom? My father explained that the city of Amman was once called Philadelphia, city of brotherly love, by the Greeks. It was one of the Decapolis, the ten federated cities the Greeks built in the region on the heels of Alexander the Great's conquests. The Romans who followed built the beautiful theater. Inside the Philadelphia Hotel, with its mahogany wall panels and deep plush rugs, it was calm and cool, a welcome respite from the heat and tumult of the world outside. Waiters wearing black tuxedos served cold lemonade.

Late that afternoon, when a light breeze began to cool the air, my father announced that it was time to visit the emir. He took me to a tent pitched on a hill near the palace, where Abdullah was holding an informal gathering. We met a few of my father's acquaintances who were sitting on the floor, smoking leisurely. They all stood up when the emir entered, and rushed toward him to kiss his hand. My father shook the emir's hand.

The monarch sat down on the floor, crossing his legs, and the guests followed suit, seating themselves in a circle. I remembered being told once that the Bedouin sat on the floor of the tent to symbolize the equality of men. No man claimed a higher position by sitting on a higher plane, including the chief. Coffee was served by two Sudanese waiters dressed in ankle-length white shirts and red vests embroidered in black and gold, their heads covered with the traditional red and white headcloth. They carried steaming brass coffeepots in one hand and trays of sweets in the other, and remained there, filling and refilling seemingly endless cups of the bitter dark drink and passing around the sugary treats. The conversation was essentially one-way. Abdullah held his guests' interest, or at least was led to believe so by the frequents nods and grunts of consent. I remembered my father telling us that he was called "the king with a twinkle in his eye." That day the twinkle was abundantly evident.

I sat next to my father, mostly ignored, unable to understand what was being said, but impressed by the appliquéd animals and flowers decorating the walls of the tent and the colorful rugs scattered on the ground. I understand now what I didn't then — that the presence of a woman in the royal tent was a deviation from tradition and a special privilege accorded to my father. Arab women were usually married or "promised" at my age. Some already had a child. None were included in men's affairs.

After my trip to Amman, other members of our family

followed, and we came to accept crossing the Jordan as a fact of life, until one day it all came to a sudden end. The friendship between King Abdullah and my father terminated abruptly in 1947, shortly before the Arab nations invaded the new state of Israel. My father made it out of Amman on the eve of the war, never to return. Within a day of Israel's declaration of statehood, Jordan, Syria, Lebanon, Iraq, and Egypt invaded Israel from all directions. King Abdullah and his army joined the Arab forces, and my father joined the Israeli Defense Force to fight Abdullah's army. The Jordanian Arab Legion took Jerusalem's Old City, destroying its ancient synagogues and cemeteries and taking many Jews prisoner. The New City was under siege, pounded by Jordanian batteries from all sides. Our house and my father's factory were hit and badly damaged. A shell penetrated several walls of our home and smashed an old grandfather clock that had been passed down from one generation to another, miraculously missing my deaf grandfather, who was sitting in the house oblivious to the sounds of war.

Word reached my father by way of his friend the Armenian patriarch of Jerusalem, who was one of the few people able to cross the borders separating Arabs and Jews, that Abdullah had issued an order to the commander of the Arab Legion to spare two houses during the attack on Jerusalem — the homes of Mendel Cohen and Doctor Avraham Ticho, the Jewish ophthalmologist who had served the king and his family. The communiqué further indicated that should these homes be accidentally damaged, the Jordanian government would pay reparations. The order didn't do much good, as the shells screeching above our heads failed to discriminate between one house and another.

When my father looked at the gaping holes in our walls he announced, "We don't need their reparations," adding in Arabic, "*Ill faht maht*" — that which is past is dead. Secretly, however, he continued his friendship with Abdullah: he committed to writing the story of his experiences at the Hashemite royal court and the events that followed.

We discovered my father's notes during one of our visits to Israel, when my husband and I were told by my uncle that he had something to show us. He took out a box filled with handwritten papers and said that they had been given to him by my late father. He had no explanation why he had been selected to be the keeper of that package, nor any idea as to its purpose, but he thought that we would find the material interesting.

We read the manuscript from start to finish in one night. Then we showed it to Hanoch Bartov, one of Israel's leading writers, who also read it in one sitting. We agreed that the material would be of enormous interest to the Israeli public, and Bartov saw to its publication. It appeared in Hebrew in 1980 under the title *At the Court of King Abdullah* and sold out within a matter of a few months.

I had been contemplating finding a publisher in America, but did not undertake the job until fifteen years later. There were always good reasons for the delay, such as managing a home and career, but lately I have come to realize that a more fundamental factor was causing my reluctance. Perhaps it was the same reason my father had been reluctant to publish his work in the first place.

After four major wars and endless bloody confrontations between Israel and her Arab neighbors, my father's stories seemed like an aberration, a lonely chord in the ca-

cophony of war, a hollow promise. How futile to go back in
time and sing the praises of a unique and unlikely friendship
that could not survive enmity and bloodshed. It was a broken bridge.

Recent changes have made me take another look at my
father's story. On October 26, 1994, Jordan and Israel signed
a treaty that made peace between the people living on the
two sides of the Jordan River a reality. Clandestine economic relations, which had been in existence for decades,
became open, tourism flourished, and new friendships between people living on opposite sides of the river were being formed.

As I was watching the signing ceremonies on television,
I began to think that my father's bittersweet experiences at
King Abdullah's court may have been more than an aberration, may rather have been one thread in a tapestry of peace,
part of a compelling human need to reach out and find a
common language. The thought grew in me that perhaps
earlier attempts to reach accommodation were in fact not
failures but part of a slow and complex process of building
peace, and that my father might have played a role in it, a
role that was peripheral in political terms but central to the
essence of peace.

President Clinton's eloquent words during the ceremony marking the signing of the peace agreement echoed
my sentiment:

> King Hussein, today in this arid place you bring to full
> flower the memories of the man who taught you to seek
> peace, your grandfather King Abdullah. When he was
> martyred four decades ago, he left you with a great

burden and a great dream. He believed that one day on both sides of the river Jordan, Arabs and Jews would live in peace. How bravely you have shouldered that burden and carried that dream. Now after so much danger and so much hardship, Your Majesty, your day has come. Truly you have fulfilled your grandfather's legacy.

I knew it was time for me to retell my father's story in the context of that legacy.

Part I

Between Jerusalem and Amman

Mendel Cohen's Story

1

The Death of a Monarch

LATE ON THE FRIDAY MORNING OF JULY 20, 1951, as the sun was about to reach its zenith and begin its slow descent behind the blue-gray hills of Jerusalem, I was beginning to feel the frenzy of the week slowly give way to the sanctity of the Sabbath. From my office on the second floor of the workshop I could hear the sounds of hammers and drills diminish — the machines were being turned off one by one in the main workroom downstairs. Soon the carpenters, finishers, porters, and apprentices would appear at my door to receive their weekly wages and bid me a good Sabbath. They would then scatter, each to his own corner of the city, some stopping to buy flowers or a bottle of wine for the Sabbath table, the more devout to assemble in ritual bathhouses to cleanse their bodies in preparation for Sabbath, the Queen.

As I was closing shop for the week, I became aware of a faint monotonous chant emanating from the radio on my desk. The dial was set to the East Jerusalem broadcasting station, transmitting the Friday Muslim prayers from the great mosque called el-Aqsa on the Temple Mount. I used to listen to these services with a sense of nostalgia tinged with sadness. They reminded me of the time when Jewish prayers, Muslim chants, and Christian church bells resonated through the courtyards and alleys of Jerusalem's Old City in a synergy of rhythm and sound. It had been only three years since the Old City was captured by Jordanian forces, the Jews expelled and the sound of their ancient prayers silenced.

Suddenly I was jolted by the sound of a gunshot on the radio, followed by rounds of gunfire and screams of agony, while the mosque reader continued his recitation of the Koran in the background. I quickly turned the dial to the Voice of Israel and sat in shock as the reports came through. I heard that King Abdullah had been shot as he entered the silver-domed mosque across from the golden Dome of the Rock, and was presumed dead. King Abdullah's grandson Hussein was also hit but miraculously survived. The assassin was shot and killed in the mosque by King Abdullah's guard. Believed to be an Arab extremist, he was found to be wearing a talisman saying "Kill and thou shalt be saved."

The news that followed came in bits and pieces, a mixture of fact and rumor, with no way to tell them apart. Interpretations abounded, variously attributing the assassination to the British, the Egyptians, and the Saudis. Some believed that the murder had been carried out by Palestinian extremists in protest against Abdullah's annexation of the West Bank of Palestine to Jordan. Others voiced the belief that the grand mufti of Jerusalem, Hajj Amin el-Husseini, Abdullah's archenemy, had been behind the assassination.

I felt as if the earth were shaking under my feet. My

first impulse was to rush to the Old City and see for myself, then I remembered that it was separated from me by barbed wire and soldiers. A wave of sadness engulfed me as I thought about the loss of the man who had played a major role not only in the history of Jordan and Israel but in my own life.

In the days that followed the assassination, memories and questions kept crowding my mind. I remembered my first meeting with the self-assured monarch, who had been my living proof that Jews and Arabs were capable of forming ties of friendship and mutual trust. I remembered the hours we had spent together playing chess, planning projects, and sharing ideas. I also thought of moments when an impassable gulf seemed to separate us, each of us cautiously avoiding getting too close to it. Particularly painful was the memory of my final departure from Jordan, when impending war had prevented us from bidding farewell to each other. We began as friends and ended up on opposite sides of a battlefield.

I had always hoped that Israel and Jordan would find a way to coexist and foster mutual cooperation, and I had often entertained the fantasy that King Abdullah and I would meet again some day and resume our friendship. The assassination shattered all hopes for renewal.

Questions began haunting me. Had I really known this complex man? Why had the king sought my friendship, and was that friendship real or illusory? Why had I stayed in Amman for ten years? Were those long days and lonely nights in a foreign land worth the sacrifice? My Jordanian venture had been a promising business opportunity as well as a chance to experience a different world, but I am slowly coming to realize that beneath these lay an unnamable longing.

I turned to the notes I had collected haphazardly during my stay in Amman to see whether they would provide some answers. Poring over pages and handwritten scraps recorded in haste, I decided to set the material in order, seeking a coherence. My casual acceptance of a construction job in Amman may have been driven by more than material needs — my daily commerce with wood and stone may have concealed the promise and yearning for something I could not make concrete.

There were striking parallels in the courses of our lives, Abdullah's and mine. We grew up in holy cities where great religions were born, he in Mecca and I in Jerusalem. Our first encounter with the written word came through the holy books, his the Koran and mine the Bible. We reached adulthood at a time of great national awakening and witnessed the evolution of our respective national movements, his Arab nationalism and mine Zionism. And this is where the similarity ends, he being born a prince and I the son of craftsmen and farmers.

As I grew up in Jerusalem at the dawn of the twentieth century, my daily life had been closely intertwined with my Arab neighbors. My first two languages were Yiddish and Arabic; Hebrew emerged as my main language only much later. The market near my house, where Arab vendors sold their produce, was my first playground. It was there that I met my first Arab friends, children of farmers who used to accompany their fathers with their goods. With them I

shared innocent childhood games of tag and marbles, sometimes laced with taunting and hat snatching.

On my daily trip to school through the heart of the Old
City, I became familiar with the hawking cries of each of the
shopkeepers along the bazaar, with the riders of donkeys
who would call out for pedestrians to make way, and with
Arab children who would alternately engage me in friendly
conversation and aim at me their juicy curses when, in my
shyness, I would avert my eyes while they unabashedly
stared at the young women passing by.

As an adult I came into close contact with my Arab
neighbors through my business. Among my Arab employees
were highly skilled carpenters and masons who hewed beautiful stones from quarries on the outskirts of Jerusalem. I enjoyed their hospitality and good humor, their music and
their colorful language spiked with verse and metaphor.

But another part of me was wary and angry. Pogroms in
Jaffa and Hebron, killing scores of innocent Jewish men,
women, and children, and growing Arab militancy and violence spurred by Hajj Amin el-Husseini, were daily threatening our lives. And when the Arab nations, with King
Abdullah as commander in chief, invaded the young state of
Israel, my hopes for a harmonious relationship with my
neighbors reached their lowest ebb.

After the war I heard of secret negotiations between
Abdullah and the Israeli government, and I hoped that the
man who had the capacity to transcend differences might
hold the key to peace. But now that Abdullah is dead and the
succession unstable, there seems no other Arab leader who
might prevent another round of bloodshed and mayhem.

There is truth to the notion that reality is far more fabulous than the most wondrous fable. My encounter with King Abdullah is proof. Serendipity? Perhaps. Perhaps not. Had a mysterious cause brought us together? Perhaps one day my children and grandchildren may read my story and with a more objective eye better understand the meaning behind it. For them, and for others who may help restore peace, I will tell the story of my adventures at the court of King Abdullah.

2

Meeting the King

I MET KING ABDULLAH at the home of Sir Arthur Wau-chope, the British high commissioner of Palestine, in 1937. Having done some construction work for the high commissioner in the past, I was hired to oversee the packing and shipping of his entire household in preparation for his retirement to his estate in Scotland. I had done this before for other British officials, but this assignment was unique, both because of the nature of Sir Arthur's possessions and the course of events that followed.

The high commissioner was a most unusual man. He was a retired general and world traveler, a gentleman of exquisite taste and refinement. His official residence, built on a hilltop in south Jerusalem and visible from many parts of the city, was made of gleaming white stone. The interior, known to only the select, was even more spectacular.

Sir Arthur's large art collection, amassed during his travels, was rich in paintings, tapestries, statues, rugs, porcelain, and antique furniture. I undertook the job of preparing that precious collection for an overseas voyage, a job that took weeks to complete and required the utmost care and precision. The cellar held hundreds of bottles of rare wine.

Sending them home by ship necessitated skillful packing, all of which was done — and done well — by my crew under the watchful eye of the high commissioner himself.

Sir Arthur's library included rare books and documents as well as contemporary works of literature in many languages. Some were written in Hebrew and were personally inscribed by their authors. Most impressive was his collection of Arabic literature. A student of the Arabic language and culture, Sir Arthur collected everything from Arab poetry to books about Middle Eastern politics.

The high commissioner's shoes were a source of wonder and amusement to me and my crew. Most of us owned only two pairs of shoes, one for work and one for formal occasions, and found his collection an unbelievable sight. An entire room was lined from floor to ceiling with shelves, containing shoes of every possible style. From the perspective of the early Jewish settlers of Israel, who believed in austerity and egalitarianism, this room struck us as another example of the excesses of the British Empire.

One object about to be packed caught my attention. It was a silver statue, ten inches high, of an Arab warrior riding a horse, wearing a traditional Arabian caftan, headdress, and dagger. With the signature of Abdullah ibn (son of) Hussein engraved on its side, it was obviously a gift given to the high commissioner by his friend the emir Abdullah of Transjordan. As I was later to discover, it was the type of gift Abdullah would offer to many of his friends and supporters. While I was admiring the piece, a group of Arab men walked into the large reception room. At the head of the group was a man I recognized to be the emir himself. He had come to bid farewell to Sir Arthur on the eve of his departure.

The large reception room was already stripped of its furnishings, and the floor, which had been covered with Persian rugs, was bare. As the emir walked into the room, he stopped suddenly and exclaimed, "All my life I have wanted a floor such as this." He told Sir Arthur of his various attempts to have such a parquet floor built, and his frustrations with the poor workmanship he had encountered.

"I could have saved you a lot of trouble had I known," replied Sir Arthur, "but if you want, you can meet the man who built it. He happens to be working in the next room."

I was called in to meet the high commissioner's guests and presented to the man sitting in a comfortable armchair sipping black coffee. He was the sovereign of Transjordan, known for his opposition to Jewish immigration to Palestine.

The emir wasted no time in getting down to business. The first question he asked was whether I spoke Arabic. He smiled pleasantly when I responded in his own tongue. It was obvious that he would converse in no language other than Arabic, take it or leave it. He immediately informed me that he liked the parquet floor I had built for the high commissioner and wanted one just like it installed at his palace in Amman.

I indicated my willingness to come to Amman, then suddenly became unsure that my response was altogether wise. Not only was I in the middle of attending to other business, I knew there were dangers in traveling to Amman. These were second thoughts, however. I was too intrigued to forgo such a rare adventure and decided to take a chance.

Emir Abdullah said he would send a car to bring me to Amman. No date was set and no details were offered. Weeks went by and no car came to fetch me, nor was there any word from the emir. I attributed the emir's offer to a passing royal whim and gave it no further thought.

Then one day, when I was in the process of completing the construction of a police station near Tel Aviv, I received an urgent phone call from Amman. One of Abdullah's emissaries informed me that the emir wished me to come to Amman and that a car was waiting in Jerusalem ready to escort me there without delay. On my return to Jerusalem, I found at the entrance to my workshop a luxury car bearing the royal Hashemite emblem. Three men were dozing in the car. I recognized them as Circassians by their long-skirted coats, high leather boots, and Astrakhan fur hats. The Circassians were Muslims who originated in the Caucasus and arrived in Transjordan in the 1880s. They were exiled by the Russian czar when he conquered their land and they came to live under the protection of the Turkish sultan. A group of some five hundred Circassians settled among the ruins of the Roman theater in Amman. As they flourished, they established other villages throughout Transjordan and became Abdullah's most trustworthy citizens. When Abdullah first arrived in Amman in 1921, the leader of the Circassian community received him with open arms and turned his home over to him. The emir and the Circassian community developed a friendship that had never abated.

The driver greeted me with expansive Middle Eastern deference and said that "Sayidna" — the designation given to the tribal chief, namely the emir — was sending his greetings and was waiting for me in Amman "regarding the matter of the parquet." I joined them willingly, confident that the emir's most trustworthy guards would do all in their power to ensure my safety.

Arab riots and attacks on the Jewish community in Palestine had peaked in 1937. Hajj Amin el-Husseini, the grand mufti of Jerusalem and the most vehement opponent to Jewish settlement in Palestine, was intensifying his venomous anti-Jewish propaganda, spurring violent attacks on the Jewish population. The mufti's influence was spreading to other Arab countries, including Transjordan.

Emir Abdullah's stance toward the Jews was more moderate than that of the mufti, and many of his citizens shared his position. Transjordan, however, had its share of extreme nationalists who had no tolerance for Jews entering their country, let alone doing business with their leader. I knew the perils involved in forming business connections with the emir, but the pull to explore the other side of the Jordan River was too great to resist. I joined the emir's guards on my first trip to Amman.

We crossed the Allenby Bridge, the major crossing point between Transjordan and Israel, without inspection, and rode to Amman by way of a back road rarely traveled by the general public. Secrecy was necessary to insure not only my own safety but, more important, that of the emir. In a region where political assassinations were common, it was not inconceivable that the mufti's followers in Transjordan might use Abdullah's business dealings with the Jews as justification to take his life, and possibly mine in the process.

As we were approaching the palace by way of the

unpaved back road, I was thinking about the circuitous paths friendships and animosities seem to take in this Holy Land of ours. I was not the first craftsman to enter into a business relationship with a prominent Arab. My father, one of the most able carpenters in old Jerusalem, had lived in friendship and harmony with the mufti's father and had built the furniture for his house, the very house in which Hajj Amin, the current mufti, grew up. The two elders used to spend time together, enjoying a cup of coffee and the view of the rolling hills of Jerusalem. The friendship was not passed on to their sons. So there I was, secretly approaching Amman, hidden from view, wondering how a friendship between fathers had turned into animosity between sons.

As we drove on, I was preoccupied by a more fundamental question. Why would the emir risk his own life and the life of others for a parquet floor? Was it the whim of a capricious and irresponsible monarch who believed he must have it all? Were we putting our lives on the line to satisfy the vagaries of a man who was no friend to my people? Later, as I came to know Abdullah better, I began to understand that my invitation to Amman was only part of a plan far greater than the installation of a parquet floor.

When we arrived at the palace, I noticed that security precautions were more relaxed and that our arrival did not come as a surprise to the people at the court. I subsequently learned that ours was one of several business connections Abdullah had sought with Palestinian Jews. One such "joint venture" took place between the emir and Pinhas Rutenberg, an engineer responsible for developing a hydraulic power plant in Palestine. An agreement between Rutenberg and Abdullah provided Rutenberg with a piece of land east of the Jordan River to expand his plant and deliver electrical power to Transjordan. Another venture concerned an agreement between Abdullah and the Palestine Potash Company for the exploitation of the Dead Sea's chemical resources.

One of the most curious episodes in Hashemite-Jewish collaboration occurred in 1933, only four years prior to my arrival in Amman, and involved twenty thousand acres of undeveloped land privately owned by Abdullah. Pressed by chronic financial shortfall, he sought investors to lease the land. The only group interested in the deal was the Jewish-held Palestine Land Development Company, which was ready to invest substantial sums of money to develop the area. The plan had the backing of a number of major tribal chiefs who were also interested in putting up their own land for lease or sale to Jewish investors. Reactions from other Arab neighbors, particularly Palestinian Arabs, however, were loud and vehement. Abdullah was accused of selling his country for money, of opening the floodgates of Transjordan to Jews, and thus of betraying the Arab national cause.

In the end it was the British who put an end to Abdullah's venture. They resurrected an old nationality law that prohibited the leasing or selling of land to noncitizens. Ironically, Transjordan, which shares the longest border with Israel and was always the most moderate country in its dealings with Israel, thus remained the only Arab neighbor to exclude all Jews from living within its borders.

Abdullah's setback in this venture did not diminish his conviction that his small and underdeveloped country would never wake up from its slumber if it failed to adopt some of the technological advances of modern nations. He was particularly impressed by the Jewish farmers on the other side of the Jordan who were turning marshes and deserts into fertile oases. As I came to discover, he greatly admired the work ethic of the Palestinian Jews and was eager to learn the secret of our success. He used to say that "God scattered the Jews to learn and spread their knowledge among the nations." I may have been one of those "scattered Jews" sought by Abdullah to assist in his modernization effort. But when I first arrived in Amman "on the matter of the parquet," I had no idea that Abdullah had more than parquet in mind and that I would spend more than ten years of my life in and out of his court.

3

At the Palace

AT THE PALACE I was greeted by Mohammed Zubati, court manager and Abdullah's confidant. He wore a striped caftan, a golden band around his headdress, and, in the manner typical of Bedouin warriors, a dagger at his waist. He was not a native of the area and his origins were obscure. I subsequently found out that no one at court knew exactly where he came from or how he got to be the monarch's right-hand man. He did not look like other Arabs at the court: he was quite a bit taller and leaner, and unlike most other men, who kept their hair hidden under their headdresses, he wore his in long black braids that hung down his shoulders. His exotic attire admitted touches of current European fashion. Over his caftan he wore a well-tailored Western sports jacket, adorned by a variety of gold pens in his breast pocket. Next to Zubati stood Mr. Azar, a Christian from Nazareth who served as court treasurer. The two gentlemen constituted an inseparable team on matters of business.

So there we were, a Muslim, a Christian, and yours truly, a Jew, working together, trying to iron out the details of a business deal on behalf of the son of Hussein ibn Ali, the grand sharif of Mecca, the ruler of the Hejaz.

The two gentlemen led me up the stairs to the main hall of the palace, where the parquet was to be laid. They showed me a set of prints submitted by an architect, apparently assuming that I would execute the plan already in existence. The discussion that followed did little to clarify matters, or to prepare me for what was to come next — a face-to-face meeting with the emir that almost ended in fiasco.

Abdullah walked in smiling calmly, looking confident that events would turn out well. He shook my hand as if he had known me for a long time and proceeded to express his thoughts about the existing plan. When he paused to ask for my opinion, a matter of formality only, I responded honestly (and, in retrospect, rather naively) that his plan could not be adequately carried out because it did not fit the existing layout of the room. He did not stop to ask for an explanation but instead responded angrily, "I want it to be done and I don't want you to tell me otherwise. You must find a way to do it." And with those words he abruptly left the room.

Years later, when we had developed a closer relationship, Abdullah told me that although he was annoyed by my failure to see things his way, I had gained his respect at that moment. He was used to another type of response from people working for him who would always say *"Hader, ya sayidi"* — at your command, master — but rarely comply. No one had had the courage to tell him what they really thought. My response both surprised him and led him to put trust in my word.

After Abdullah left, the two men rushed to give me a quick course in communication with Sayidna. They shared with me the essence of the rules of the game. "You must remember," they said, "that if he says that black is white, you must agree with him, or at least say that black is white but has a little black in it. You must never disagree with him categorically."

I did not see Abdullah again that day, but I sent word through his emissaries that I would get the job done to the best of my ability, and offered to prepare a miniature model of the room with a parquet floor sample for his examination. He was appeased and agreed to look at a prepared model, so long as it was submitted within a reasonable time. I agreed to have it completed within a week.

After lunch with his two officials I returned to Jerusalem, again under the protection of the Circassian guards. The model was prepared within a few days, but a whole month went by and no one came to pick it up. Again I decided to give little practical significance to the encounter in Amman, attributing it to the emir's flight of fancy. However, I didn't regret the experience. It had been full of novelty and suspense and valuable in and of itself.

A few weeks later, having received no further communication, I was again summarily summoned to Amman to finalize the agreement on the installation of the floor.

Carrying the model of the parquet floor, I was driven to Amman in an armored car. The emir greeted me with a warm handshake and invited me to join him for lunch. Seated at the table were the two gentlemen I had met earlier, Mr. Zubati and Mr. Azar. Also at the table were Prime Minister Tawfiq Abul Huda, Abdullah's private physician

Dr. Shukat, and Usni Pasha, one of Abdullah's closest friends, later to become his private secretary. Sitting next to his father was Prince Naif, Abdullah's younger son, who followed his footsteps like a shadow. Abdullah's older son Talal was absent; he had been banished to Baghdad a few months earlier, following a severe altercation with his father.

During the meal Abdullah entertained the guests with stories and jokes, rarely referring to issues directly. I sensed that he meant to convey more than simply entertaining episodes, but had not yet mastered the art of indirect language. I wasn't quite sure whether the people seated around the table understood him either, though they frequently nodded their heads in approval. I saw a half-grin of satisfaction on Abdullah's face when he noticed their puzzled looks.

Abdullah expressed pleasure at the fact that he did not need a translator in dealing with me, and that we could communicate directly in his native language. Even the British, he commented with pride, had to speak to him in Arabic. He further added that he intended to supervise our work personally, a statement that accurately foretold the nature of things to come.

At the end of the meal Abdullah indicated satisfaction with the model I had built and informed me that he was ready to offer me the job. He insisted, however, that the work be completed before the onset of Ramadan, a month of fasting and prayer. On the eve of Ramadan it was customary for the emir to receive distinguished guests who had come to pay homage and to wish him well, kissing his hand and bestowing on him the blessing "Every year will bring you peace." That year, Abdullah wanted the reception to take place in the Great Hall, where the parquet floor was to be installed. He then left me with Mr. Zubati, the court manager, and Mr. Azar, the court treasurer, to work out final arrangements.

The gaiety that had characterized the meal disappeared as soon as the grueling process of bartering had begun. In their effort to demonstrate loyalty to their superior, the two men used every trick in the book to negotiate the lowest possible price. In the Middle East, the art of bartering is essential to all commercial transactions. Both buyer and seller try to use their *shatara*, a mixture of shrewdness, mettle, and mental agility, in pursuit of the best possible deal. As an Arab proverb says: "The true art of bartering occurs during the deal-making, not after." Zubati and Azar were undeniable experts in the art. That afternoon they demonstrated an extraordinary degree of expertise, one that surpassed anything I'd experienced before.

Though I had lived in the Middle East all my life, and had conducted business there for more than half my life, I never acquired a taste for this type of exchange. I preferred to offer my customers a fair price — which they usually accepted. Approaching this job in the same manner, I had itemized my estimate and assumed that any agreement would include acceptance of the fixed costs. This was not the understanding of the two gentlemen, however. Their way of conducting business was altogether different from mine.

Negotiations began with the question "Sayidna is asking how much of the cost you are willing to forgive in his honor." Messages were delivered in the name of Sayidna whenever convenient. His assistants around the court swore and even lied in the name of the emir, often without his awareness or authorization. They used the term "forgive" to suggest that the matter of actual cost was not the issue. On the contrary, they acknowledged that my estimate was fair and the product deserving of its cost, but were asking for a personal concession — my readiness to forgive and forgo part of the profit out of respect for Sayidna.

I told them that my policy was to quote a fair price and to stand by it, a statement they either failed to understand or were unwilling to accept. "This has never happened to us before!" they exclaimed. "You must forgo some of your price to show Sayidna your respect." They insisted on a reduction, however small. At stake was their own pride, proof of their ability to conduct business in a skillful manner. They haggled for an increasingly smaller price cut. First they asked for 15 percent, then 10, and finally reduced it to 5 percent. I stood firm and insisted on the sum named in my original proposal.

The men began to wonder whether I was actually interested in the job. In their business world, refusal to bargain was viewed as a sign that one wished to bail out of the deal. Mr. Zubati and Mr. Azar therefore construed my inflexibility as an attempt to withdraw from the project, a prospect they could not entertain, knowing that Abdullah was determined to have the floor built. They were visibly distressed. How were they going to face Sayidna with no results? "You are endangering our very existence!" they opined. They promised to give me additional work at higher pay, if only I would be willing to show some "forgiveness." That way they would be able to go back to their master with some sort of deal. I didn't budge. I knew that additional rounds of bargaining and changes in conditions would ensue — that it would come back to haunt me if I didn't stand my ground. As much as I needed to be on good terms with these men, I would get lost in the complex maze of the Arab marketplace unless I could undertake the work on my own terms.

Mr. Zubati and Mr. Azar had no choice but to return to the emir empty-handed. Abdullah, partly puzzled and partly annoyed, decided to intervene directly. He entered the room and, in a voice intended to be heard by all present, announced, "I have never heard of a man who won't forgive anything. Why can't you cooperate and get on with the job?" Then he left the room. It was evident that he had no intention of entering into negotiations with me, as it was not befitting his role. He turned the task back to his two surrogates, who succumbed. "You win," they said. "Just be sure to get the job done by Ramadan."

The treasurer was ordered to pay me an advance, but the check had to be signed by Mr. Zubati. Mr. Azar filled in the amount and Mr. Zubati propped the check on his knee and signed it with great effort. He handed it to me with the reminder, "Don't forget us." In Europe, the payment to which he alluded would be called a "kickback." In the Middle East it is known as *bakhshish*.

4

Getting Acquainted

THREE DAYS LATER, BEFORE DAWN, two large trucks appeared at the entrance to my workshop in Jerusalem. I selected a team of six skilled young craftsmen who were eager to try something new and were prepared to be away from home for several weeks. Among them were my two youngest brothers, Avraham and Yonah. They were to prove invaluable in the days to come. We succeeded in loading the vehicles and reaching Amman just as the sun began to appear over the Syrian Desert. Except for the sound of Abdullah chanting the morning prayers the court was silent. Everyone knew that Sayidna must not be interrupted during his prayers. *"Sayidna be ikra"* meant that the master was reading the Koran. No worldly matter could be brought to his attention at that time.

Abdullah's morning schedule followed a regular routine. After prayer he stopped at the quarters of the Great Emira, his first wife and mother of his first-born son, Talal. She lived in her own separate wing of Raghdan Palace. Next came the visit to the Minor Emira, mother of Naif, his second son. She lived in the opposite wing of the palace. The obligatory morning visits to the harem accomplished, Ab-

dullah would step out to review the palace guard and partic-
ipate in the flag-raising ceremony. A large black Mercedes-
Benz, bearing the royal emblem and the national flag, would
then bring him to yet another stop, the home of his young
concubine, Nahada, later to become his third wife, who
lived in quarters away from the royal palace. From there Abdullah would be driven to the Diwan, the house of government and his official office. All this would take place before
the clock struck seven.

On this particular morning Abdullah was up earlier
than usual. He came by to inspect the progress of the work
and to meet the men who had arrived with me from
Jerusalem. He appeared surprised and somewhat disappointed when he realized that the foundation of the floor
was about to be completed. "You have hardly removed the
dust from your shoes, and you are already dipping your feet
in the cement! What is the big hurry?" he asked. Had he
forgotten his earlier admonition about completing the work
on time? When we had first met at the palace of the high
commissioner in Jerusalem, Abdullah expressed dismay at
the languid pace at which things were done in his country,
but that morning, when he saw us at work, he did not seem
pleased.

Our energetic pace led Abdullah to suspect that we
were doing a shoddy job. He stood there scrutinizing our
work, not sure whether to admire or criticize it. I realized
that he wanted to be involved, and decided to include him in
the details of the job, much to his satisfaction. In appreciation of the fact that my men had begun work before breakfast, he ordered his kitchen staff to prepare a festive midday
meal for us.

It was from that moment on that Abdullah began to address me as the *muhandes*, the engineer. He meant it as a title of distinction, to confer his recognition of someone possessing a high level of technological skill. He followed our progress with great interest, demonstrating an understanding of construction that I found surprising. I sensed that he was pleased with our work, but I did not expect at the time that he would become personally interested in my welfare or in the welfare of my workers.

Abdullah joined us again after our meal and shook hands with the workers. He wanted to know the names of each and every one of them. The first man he spoke to was named Zvi. When I explained that the name meant "deer" in Hebrew, Abdullah's face lit up. He told us it was also an Arab custom to name people after an animal, so that they would reflect its qualities. Men were given names of fierce animals to inspire them with courage and boldness, women names of tame animals to prepare them for servitude and domesticity. He thought the name Zvi fit this alert young man. "You are quick and quiet, like a deer in the field," he told him.

Abdullah liked the Biblical names of some of the workers. The names were familiar, Joseph being Yusuf in Arabic, Avraham equivalent to Ibrahim in his native tongue, and Yonah, which is akin to the Arabic Yunah. He was delighted to discover that they appeared in both the Koran and the Bible.

When Abdullah heard that one man in our crew was named Weitzmann he began talking about Dr. Chaim Weizmann, president of the Zionist World Organization and one of the most influential figures in world Jewry. Weizmann and Abdullah represented opposite ends of the spectrum with regard to the future of Palestine. While Weizmann strove to establish a Jewish state in Palestine, Abdullah harbored dreams of forming a unified Arab state under his sovereignty comprising both Transjordan and Palestine. In 1922, in an attempt to find a resolution to the Arab-Jewish conflict, a meeting between Weizmann and Abdullah was held in London. Abdullah offered the Jewish community autonomy over a small area of Palestine if they assisted him in unifying both sides of the Jordan River. This position, subsequently offered by Abdullah time and again, was consistently rejected by the Jewish community, for it was incongruent with its national aspirations. Political differences notwithstanding, Abdullah had much to say in praise of Weizmann. "We Arabs don't have a leader such as yours," he said with sadness and envy. "I hope that one day we will have our own Weizmann."

Abdullah was particularly interested in one of the youngest men in the group, my seventeen-year-old brother Avraham. Avraham spoke fluent Arabic and was a highly efficient worker. One day, while watching him working, Abdullah remarked, "From the way you work I can tell that one day you will be a great builder." Abdullah's prophecy came true. My brother eventually became chief supervisor of a number of construction projects for the emir. Abdullah used to boast that Avraham had grown to become a man and master builder while at the royal court. But my brother learned about more than construction at Abdullah's court. The seeds of Avraham's international career were probably planted during the ten years he spent in Abdullah's domain. Mastery of the Arabic language, knowledge of Arab culture and history, and, perhaps most important, experience with the internal dynamics of the court gave Avraham tools that he used with great skill later in life. The emir never lived to see Avraham become an expert in Islamic and Middle Eastern studies, as well as an accomplished statesman and ambassador.

Moshe was the last man to shake hands with the emir that day. The name Moshe aroused the emir's interest, for it was equivalent to Musah, the Arab name for Moses, who was also a major prophet to Islam. Abdullah inquired where Moshe had come from. Moshe responded that he came from Poland. "And what brought you to Palestine?" Abdullah asked. "My desire to live in the land of my forefathers and build it," replied the man, without thinking of the touchy content of his statement. I expected Abdullah to bristle. Moshe was proclaiming his commitment to the Zionist cause, which was at odds with Hashemite ambitions. But when I translated the man's words into Arabic, Abdullah did not seem at all offended. He continued to ask questions about Moshe's family and their whereabouts. Moshe explained that his wife and child were still in Poland, awaiting receipt of a certificate to enter Palestine. They were being held back by the British government.

The emir understood quite well why Moshe's wife and son could not join him in Palestine. Despite the Balfour Declaration which supported the establishment of a Jewish homeland, Britain was imposing severe restrictions on Jewish immigration. This policy remained in effect throughout the Second World War and blocked the escape route of hundreds of thousands of Jews, who therefore fell victim to Nazi extermination. Abdullah himself played an important role in influencing the British into setting those limits. But he personally intervened on behalf of Moshe and his family, asking his friend the high commissioner of Palestine in Jerusalem to furnish a certificate of immigration to Moshe's wife and son, thus saving them from a Nazi death camp.

I never ceased to wonder at the dichotomy in Abdullah's attitude toward Jews. On the one hand he considered us and our settlement in Palestine one of the most serious threats to his hopes for hegemony over the Middle East and Arab control of the region. On the other, his attitude toward Jews as individuals was open and empathetic. The encounter between Abdullah and Moshe was not unique. It was one of many episodes I would come to witness.

Abdullah continued to drop by every morning to check on the progress of the work. He remembered the names of the men, often entered into brief conversation with them, and never failed to praise them for work well done. I was aware that Arab hospitality called for the offering of generous words of praise to one's guests, but Abdullah seemed to be expressing more than the conventional attitude of a host. Threads of friendship were beginning to be woven.

Inspecting the work Abdullah would often murmur, "What Allah wants is what is going to be." Were those, I always wondered, words of gratitude to Allah for things going his way? Were they words of regret, asking forgiveness for being swayed by the West? After all, if he strayed, wasn't that also the will of Allah the Merciful?

5

A Royal Guided Tour

DURING MY THIRD WEEK IN AMMAN the emir invited me to venture beyond the Great Hall and join him on a tour of the palace. The purpose of the tour was not made explicit, but I didn't ask questions. I was beginning to understand that events would eventually convey their own meaning.

Raghdan Palace was built on a barren round hill, overlooking Amman on one side and the Syrian Desert on the other. The palace and its adjacent mosque had been one of Abdullah's first building projects after he established his government in Amman. The selection of the site had been a major point of contention between Abdullah and the British mandate's representative at the time, Sir Arthur Philby. To clear a site for his palace Abdullah proposed destroying a sixteenth-century Byzantine basilica, and Philby, an amateur archeologist, could not hide his repugnance at the thought. He tried to dissuade Abdullah from carrying out his plan, but to no avail. During one of their heated arguments Abdullah is said to have told Philby, "No one can stop me! Who is to tell me what to do?" This incident forever soured relations between Abdullah and Philby.

No expense was spared to make the palace both spectacular and comfortable. To the consternation of the British, the building budget was continually being augmented, and yet, owing to poor workmanship and inadequate planning, the building never acquired a finished look. At any given time one could find workmen repairing and renovating. As soon as one part of the building was completed, another needed attention. There were Druse construction workers, carpenters from Jaffa, painters from Bethlehem, and plumbers from Damascus, with no one coordinating their activities.

The architects of the original design had apparently attempted to blend Middle Eastern charm with Western convenience. It was obvious that they had failed to achieve either goal. Unlike some of the classic Arab buildings, with their arabesques, arches, and minarets, the palace was a study in confused eclecticism, characterized mostly by showy flamboyance and exaggerated features intended to catch the eye. The designers had seemed to base their work on the notion that beauty meant a gaudy mix of patterns and styles.

Abdullah, a man of excellent taste, was never satisfied with the results, and kept ordering renovations that repeatedly brought him disappointment and distress. His many experts were always ready with new plans for improvement, but usually offered contradictory suggestions. Though he kept changing architects and contractors, he could not find a solution to the aesthetic disarray of his home.

We began our tour outside. Pillars and arches painted a turquoise blue, with spiraling red stripes around them, stood at the entrance. Latticed frames adorned the large central windows, while the smaller side windows were decorated with colored lightbulbs that were lit for festive occasions. The roof was covered with an unattractive sheeting often used in factory buildings. Two old Turkish cannons were positioned at the palace door, facing the city of Amman. Next to the cannons stood two ramshackle huts, used to shelter the guards from the intense heat of the sun.

Balconies on the second floor, extending to the women's quarters, were decorated with railings made of painted concrete shaped like grape leaves. These were to keep the women from being seen, while enabling them to catch a glimpse of the world outside the harem.

As we walked into the entrance hall, I felt the coolness of the white marble fountain in its center. On the wall behind the fountain hung a very large, ornately framed distortion mirror. One side caused a reflection to appear short and fat, while the other exaggerated length. I later discovered that Abdullah had had the mirror placed in the entrance hall as a prank, characteristic of the playfulness that entertained his friends but annoyed the British no end. I eventually managed to obtain his approval to move the mirror to a less conspicuous spot in the court.

A fair-sized parlor was located to the left of the entrance hall. The walls were lined with cabinets displaying a large collection of gold and silver vessels stashed chaotically on shelves as if ready to be auctioned off. The rooms were stuffy, dusty, and dark, their walls decorated with portraits of Abdullah's father and brothers cut out of magazines and put in flimsy frames. There were cushions, deep sofas, chairs, and side tables inlaid with mother-of-pearl scattered around haphazardly without apparent attention to function or pattern. The windows were draped in heavy velvet which blocked both air and light from entering and served essentially as collectors of the dust that blew in from the surrounding desert. The windows themselves were so loosely fitted that they kept out neither the hot winds of summer nor the cold gales of winter. Looking up, I could barely make out a beautiful painted ceiling through a layer of dust. One could tell that it was an object of rare beauty, reminiscent of the painted domes and ceilings of the great churches and palaces of Europe. It differed from them, however, in one respect. The Koran prohibits the depiction of human and animal figures, so it was composed solely of colorful geometric designs.

The ground floor contained other rooms intended for conferences and were rarely used, since most official business was conducted at the Diwan in downtown Amman. Sunlight, so abundant in the region, rarely entered those rooms.

We descended a few narrow stairs to the basement, where the kitchen was located. It was spacious but minimally equipped. Most of the food preparation was done on the floor. Sitting on the floor, or squatting, was not an imposition for the cooks, who prefer these positions to sitting on chairs. I remembered once hearing that the Bedouin prefer squatting to sitting, because it permits them to get up and run if attacked by another tribe. The Bedouin I saw working in the kitchen, however, did not seem to be anticipating an attack. They conversed calmly as they peeled vegetables and cleaned the rice, changing their posture only to kneel as Sayidna walked by. A big stove fueled by wood was located in the center of the kitchen. I gasped when I saw that the wood being used as fuel came from fruit-bearing trees, so sparse and precious in that barren land. The burning of olive was particularly distressing to me, for I deeply admired the qualities of that wood. Two huge brass platters, one approximately ten feet in diameter and the other seven or eight feet, caught my eye. These large platters, Abdullah casually explained, were used on those rare occasions when a whole roasted camel was being served.

We climbed back up to the second story, where my men were at work installing the new floor. The two large wings on opposite sides of the Great Hall, occupied by Abdullah's wives, the Great Emira and the Minor Emira, were completely out of bounds to anyone except Abdullah, female guests, children, servants, and the eunuchs in charge. I had not as yet seen the women and was advised by people at court never to try. "Sayidna would shoot any man who dared look up there," they cautioned. Even raising one's eyes in the direction of the women's residence was considered a serious violation. Having been forewarned, I didn't dare raise my head in the direction of the harem as we walked by. We passed several rooms of no specified use, all darkened by heavy curtains and sparsely furnished.

The garden was in no better shape. The British government provided only a very meager budget for the upkeep of the exterior. The funds were sufficient to plant a garden but not to maintain it. Gardens were apparently used in unusual ways at the palace. I had heard it said that when Abdullah and the Saudi king Ibn Saud, lifelong enemies, were in the process of making peace, a delegation of Saudis came to Amman by camel caravan. Abdullah received his guests with lavish hospitality, providing refreshment befitting guests of such importance. The camels, which had traveled through the desert for days without food and water, were also given a special treat — they were let loose in the emir's young pine grove. Within a matter of hours not a shred of foliage was left.

The tour of the palace ended without discussion. I was learning that the bluntness so typical of Israeli discourse was alien to this environment, where meanings and messages were often conveyed in roundabout and idiosyncratic ways. I made no attempt to ask why I had been shown the palace. Events would explain all.

6

Inside the Emir's Tent

With the work moving along smoothly, I found some time to look around this new colorful world in which I had found myself. There was a great deal I wanted to understand, particularly about Emir Abdullah the man.

I didn't have long to wait. A few days after my arrival Abdullah invited me to drop in at his tent. No time was set, but I knew by then that schedules meant little in this new world, unbound as it was by clocks or calendars. Things happened when they happened. Several nights later I took Abdullah at his word.

The tent was pitched on a hill north of the palace, the expanse of the Syrian Desert on one side, patches of green pasture on the other. Horses could always be found lingering around the entrance of the tent, occasionally poking their heads inside. Abdullah knew the name of every horse and would talk to them while indulging them with sugar cubes. The tent was the place where informal court hearings, crucial political negotiations, and big *sulkha* (peacemaking) meals took place. Important guests were often entertained there, though on the evening I chose, Abdullah was receiving one of his more humble guests.

I saw the emir sitting cross-legged and leaning back on silk cushions. The spacious tent was divided into two parts, one for sleeping and the other for eating, lounging, and entertaining. Curtains serving as partitions were decorated with appliquéd figures of birds, horses, and flowers. The floor was covered with Persian rugs and sheepskins. Horse and camel saddles, decorated with red fringe, shells, and blue glass beads, as well as banners, swords, and riding crops added to the breathtaking array of color and shape.

Abdullah summoned me in and asked his servant to fetch us coffee. Following mutual greetings of peace and offering of thanks to Allah for the good fortune of health, Abdullah introduced me to the tent. A tent is called a "house of hair," he explained, because it is woven out of goat or camel hair. He himself preferred to call it the House of Allah, because its curtains could be raised on all sides to welcome all travelers, be they friend or foe.

A typical Bedouin tent consists of one long woven awning supported by pairs of poles on each side, plus a central pole serving as the main support. When desert winds swirled through, the men would hold on to the main pole to keep the tent anchored. When a major dust storm sped across the desert, of course, little could be done. The tent dwellers would sprawl on top of their belongings to keep them from flying, and cover themselves with their robes, letting the wind blow the awnings away. Modern water-repellent canvas was not as effective as hand-woven awnings made of wool, Abdullah explained. While modern canvas could withstand a normal volume of rain, it could not offer full protection against the deluge of sudden downpours that sometimes strike the region in winter. Heavy wool awnings, on the other hand, are less permeable because they shrink as they absorb the rain, preventing water from entering the tent. There are exceptions. Tents made out of goat hair from the Jordan Valley tend to let the rain in. Because of the intense heat in the valley the goats' wool is thin and sparse, unfit for weaving good tent awnings.

The tent, Abdullah further explained, is a sanctuary, offering protection to anyone who seeks refuge, including one's worst enemy. In his casual way he recounted a story about Sheikh Ibn Suweit's "little house" (tent, in Bedouin vernacular). It had happened not long before, when no rain had fallen on the desert and no grass was growing to feed the animals. A small area in a wadi retained some green, and Bedouin from all directions descended on it with their herds. Some of the tribes that gathered in the valley had been sworn enemies for centuries, and everyone knew that it would not take long before bloody fights erupted. The chiefs of the tribes understood that if old enmities prevailed, mutual extermination would ensue. They agreed on a truce for the duration of the drought, and vowed that anyone who violated the agreement would be denied sanctuary. But the inevitable happened. A fight soon erupted and a man was killed. The killer fled to the sanctuary of Sheikh Ibn Suweit's tent, held on to the central pole, and declared: "I am under the protection of this house!" Ibn Suweit sprang forward, stood between the pursuers and the killer, and refused to hand him over. The sheikhs who had taken the oath protested, "Didn't we agree to deny sanctuary to murderers, and didn't you swear with all of us?" Ibn Suweit replied: "Yes, we men took an oath, but my tent, which has always given sanctuary to the enemy, did not take the vow."

With a quiet chuckle Abdullah then told me about the dwellers of the towns of Medaba and Kerak, who decided to give up their tents and build themselves modern stone houses. By the end of the first winter they were forced to go back to their tents, because the heavy rains that came through their roofs destroyed their belongings and caused dangerous flooding. Now, he said, they leave their stone houses in the winter and come to live in their wool tents throughout the rainy season.

Abdullah also reminisced about the good old days when the entire production of wool awnings was done by women. They spun the wool, wove and shaped it into strips, and stitched the strips together into large panels. The men would then secure the awning with ropes and wooden pegs. Modern mass-produced tents, in his opinion, lacked beauty and durability.

As I listened, I was struck by the richness of the language used to describe the tent and its furnishings. I heard new words for nuances of color and texture, words describing the myriad tasks and materials involved in building a tent. Here were language and experiences totally unfamiliar to modern Western people. I felt transported back in time to the origins of my own people. Biblical images flashed through my mind. I thought of the patriarch Abraham, father of both the Jewish and the Islamic religions, who also lived in a tent open to visitors from all sides, always ready to serve hungry and thirsty travelers crossing the desert. The image of King Solomon's dark tent also crossed my mind; I was thinking about the love song from the Song of Solomon: "I am black, but comely, O ye daughters of Jerusalem, as the tents of Kedar, as the curtains of Solomon."

I felt a kinship between us that went back thousands of years.

Not long after the initial visit, I was invited to join the emir for a meal at his tent. Among the guests were his son Naif, the court physician, the minister of finance, and the court manager. The guests exchanged greetings, shook hands, and sat down on the bright carpets scattered throughout the tent. Two servants dressed in long white shirts, red embroidered vests, and tasseled red tarbooshes entered, each carrying a brass tray heaped with small cups in one hand and a brass coffeepot in the other. They kept filling the cups as soon as they were emptied, only stopping if the guest shook his cup, a sign meaning "no refill." After a few cups of bitter black coffee, the guests left the tent to wash their hands and pray in preparation for dinner. Back in the tent, they arranged themselves in a circle, some cross-legged, some squatting.

Four hefty young Sudanese servants entered the tent and placed a large brass tray in the center of the circle. A whole roasted lamb stuffed with hard-boiled eggs and vegetables lay on a mound of rice. The entire dish was covered with almonds, raisins, and bits of dried fruit. A dozen or more bowls containing salads, yogurt, green and black olives, goat cheese, meatballs cooked in sour cream, and a variety of seasoned dressings were placed around the tray. The servants drew their silver swords out of their sheaths and proceeded to slice the lamb in true Bedouin fashion. After murmuring praise for Allah, the guests tore pieces of lamb off the carcass with one hand and formed a ball of rice in the palm of their other hand. These were tossed straight into the mouth. Miraculously, the rice balls never missed their target.

Drinking water out of a clay jug was an art I had never mastered. The jug was passed around, lifted up in the air, and aimed toward the mouth, letting the water flow in the air directly into the throat without ever touching the lips. I was the object of good-humored laughter, for I repeatedly spilled the water on my face and my shirt. Grapes, figs, almond cakes, and *kanafa* — a sweet made of cream, nuts, and honey — were served as dessert. To signify the end of the meal, silver bowls filled with rose water were brought in for hand washing.

Sitting cross-legged for more than two hours was beginning to affect my back, but the other guests did not seem to mind, or if they did they did not complain. After final words of gratitude were expressed to the host, the guests dispersed. I walked out into the night with the finance minister at my side. He must have guessed at my amazement. He told me that this feast was nothing compared to some of the more lavish events. On one occasion, when the emir was entertaining members of the rival Saudi dynasty, a whole camel had been roasted kneeling in its natural position, stuffed with a whole roasted lamb and roasted chickens, and served on a huge brass platter. I had seen those huge brass trays in the palace kitchen and knew he was not exaggerating.

My visits to the tent became a frequent event. I often found Abdullah reading from the Koran, contemplating his chessboard, or listening to radio broadcasts from Palestine and other neighboring countries. We used to share our dread of a second world war, which was looming on the horizon. Abdullah's abhorrence of Hitler was clear and palpable. On this we saw eye to eye.

Only a short distance lay between the tent and the palace, but they were worlds apart. The palace was where political duties were performed, while the tent was mainly home to matters of the heart. It was a place permeated by the traditions of the vanishing Bedouin, an icon of a tribal society of camel-riding nomads for whom valor, self-sacrifice, and religious devotion comprised the essence of manhood. It was in his tent that Abdullah found relief from the modern world, and indulged in nostalgia and meditation.

I came to know the emir more familiarly in the intimacy of the tent. It was there that I first caught a glimpse of the man in his traditional setting, rooted in his Arabian heritage, freed from the dictates of Western politics. Having let me into his personal dwelling, the emir was also letting me into his private world.

7

Building Fever

THE PARQUET FLOOR IN THE GREAT HALL was finished in time for the Ramadan holiday. We worked until the very last minute, applying the finishing touches that make the difference between an acceptable product and a work of art.

Abdullah, who rarely saw a job completed to his full satisfaction, stayed with us almost continuously during the last few days, keeping his eye on the progress of the work. When the last of the tools was carried out, Abdullah sat down on his velvet-covered throne, his face beaming as he contemplated the floor. He bent down to touch it, and stroked it as he often did the silky mane of a favorite Arabian horse.

At sunset, as the room was getting darker, I suggested to Abdullah that he switch on the electric lights. The red glow of the sunset over the Syrian Desert and the lights reflecting the crystal droplets of the chandeliers sent shimmering rays onto the sparkling wooden floor. People began to arrive. It was the eve of Ramadan, when special guests came to visit their monarch, kiss his hand, and wish him well. Among the guests were the British Resident, the commander of the Arab Legion, members of the cabinet, and a host of relatives and dignitaries. Abdullah made a point of showing them around, pointing out the details of the new construction, and making special mention of the fact that the work had been done by the *yahud*, the Jews.

When the reception was over and the last of the guests had gone, Abdullah ordered tables to be set for dinner in the Great Hall and invited me and the crew to eat with him. In his usual monologue, Abdullah again recalled his disappointment with the quality of work done for him in the past and expressed his satisfaction and gratitude to my crew. By now, accustomed to his compliments, the hungry crew was primarily interested in the clang of dishes, signifying the beginning of the meal.

At the end of the meal Abdullah invited me to join him in his private office. There he told me that he wished to proceed with the renovation of the entire palace, and intimated that the tour we had taken earlier was intended to familiarize me with the condition of the structure. He also apologized for the pressure put on me by his deputies during the initial negotiations and offered to pay an additional sum in compensation. I firmly declined to change the terms of the original agreement; it was compensation enough that I no longer had to put up with the strain of bargaining each time a new project was considered.

One early object of our attention was Abdullah's private office, located off the dining room on the second floor. It was a fairly small room, but spacious enough to conduct his personal business. We built a large desk and placed it in the middle of the room and put green leather-upholstered chairs around it. A telephone, radio, globe, chess set, a musical clock that was a gift from the British Colonial Office, writing utensils, and Hashemite stationery bearing a golden crown were all neatly arranged on the desk. Shelves and files for Abdullah's personal papers were placed in cabinets along the walls. The drapes were drawn most of the time, keeping the office dark and private.

Another area where Abdullah had alterations in mind was the palace staircases. The polished white marble steps were narrow, steep, and slippery. Abdullah wanted them lowered and widened and constructed of the same wood used for the parquet floor. It would be an ambitious project because it required breaking through walls and changing some of the building's interior layout. Abdullah and I spent long hours exploring various plans, and when he finally made up his mind to proceed he insisted that the job be completed by the onset of the Beiram holiday — due to arrive in a month's time. There was no mention of cost, only a tacit understanding that I would set a fair price and that he would reimburse me in full when the work was completed. I had as much confidence in his integrity as he did in my fairness. When I said in jest that from then on there would be no middlemen to come between us, he smiled and replied, "No one is to come between us except Allah."

In the last few days before Beiram, we worked at a frantic pace. We were fortunate to be able to recruit students from a vocational school in Amman to help with polishing and cleaning. My crew worked almost twenty-four hours a day, taking turns to catch a brief nap or grab a bite of food. When the first guests began to arrive on the eve of Beiram, the last hammer blows could still be heard in the back. Then all work stopped. We left the palace through the back door and were driven home by the royal chauffeurs. I flopped into bed for a long, uninterrupted sleep.

After the holiday I saw Abdullah walking around the parlor rooms on the ground floor. The banging and hammering had ceased and the furniture was no longer covered in layers of dust, so the palace was quiet and calm. The emir, however, did not seem at peace. He was inspecting everything with great intensity and concentration, apparently contemplating his next project. This time, I took the initiative and made a suggestion based on an idea I had had for some time.

I had long been impressed with Abdullah's books, which were piled on windowsills and stacked in closets and corners. He had a rich collection of works from Teheran and Baghdad, Istanbul and Alexandria, Cairo and Damascus, Jerusalem and the great cities of Europe. Most were written in Arabic but there were others in Farsi, Turkish, Hebrew, and a host of European languages. They had been given to Abdullah by distinguished guests, and many were personally inscribed. There were books on the Koran, with decorations of every style and description; books about the Arabian, Turkish, and Persian kings; and books about the Arabian golden age in Spain. Abdullah's collection also contained material on Middle Eastern affairs, some issued by the Hebrew University of Jerusalem and others published by Arab and British sources. There were art books, novels, photo books of horses, and monographs on equestrian arts. I knew his collection well; I often browsed through it and borrowed from it for my own reading. The neglect and disdain with which it was treated pained me. I longed to put some order to its treasures.

I suggested to Abdullah that great riches were buried in the books scattered throughout the palace and that he might consider organizing them into a library — home to past, present, and future publications on the Hashemites. The idea caught his imagination. He quickly designated one of the parlors on the ground floor for the purpose. "By all means!" he told me enthusiastically. "There is no reason to hold back. Just get to it!"

The furniture in the parlor was sold off. Mohammed Zubati organized the sale and managed a small profit (which he failed to share with the original owner). The old shutters were removed from the windows, the floors dug up, and the rough cement on the walls removed and a smooth surface applied. I was able to get hold of some rather exotic wood. This was 1941, the middle of the Second World War, and the usual shipments of lumber to Palestine and Transjordan from Austria, Romania, Sweden, and Russia had come to a halt. The British needed huge amounts of lumber to build their army camps, and began to import wood from Australia, India, Burma, and Indochina. The wood came in a variety of hues and textures, affording interesting decorative possibilities. Around that same time I was building barracks for the British army in southern Palestine, using lumber imported from the Far East. I received permission from British officials to buy some of the excess for Emir Abdullah and transport it to Amman.

We built bookcases of red mahogany from India and gave them glass doors, then arranged the books. A large teak table was placed in the center of the room and surrounded by comfortable reading chairs. A leather-bound guest book was placed on top of a pedestal. In time the guest book came to include the names of commissioners, representatives, ministers, kings, and princes from around the world.

I couldn't help but notice that the library was missing a most important body of literature: Abdullah's own writings. I had heard him recite his ballads and knew of his speeches to his Parliament as well as the letters he'd written, but I didn't know whether they'd ever been published or made available to the public.

One day I saw the emir in his new library, admiring its tidy shelves and looking out the windows, through which you could see the bright sky over the Judean desert and the rugged hills of Moab. "Why did I keep these windows shuttered all these years?" he asked me, breathing deep the dry air blowing off the desert. It was then that I decided to approach him about a most private, and possibly sensitive, matter.

"*Ya sayidi,*" I began, "I hear that the Hashemites have a way with the pen. Are there any of their books or manuscripts that might be included in the library?"

"I suppose so," he responded, then walked across to his private office. He returned carrying a large cardboard box. "Here, you can read those," he said, handing me the box and abruptly walking away.

I spent many nights poring over the handwritten manuscripts. A new world was opened before me. I had seen Abdullah compose poems extemporaneously, I had heard him recite ballads and use poetic metaphor in his daily discourse, but I was not prepared for the volume of written material entrusted to my hands. The collection included poems about the Bedouin tent dwellers, their customs and mores; poems about the exquisite nobility and beauty of his favorite

Arabian horses; poems expressing his longing for his former home, the Hejaz, with its deserts and oases; poems written in praise of leaders of days past; and poems about his devotion to the Prophet and his faith. Some were short and humorous, dealing with subjects of daily life such as cars and planes and other objects of modern technology, but most were highly emotional and written in an old Arabic idiom. The box also contained copious letters, complete speeches, and outlines of speeches. I focused on material relevant to Zionism and the Jewish community in Palestine, and was amazed at the depths of subtlety it revealed. In speeches to British politicians such as the high commissioner of Palestine or the British Foreign Office, Abdullah passionately expressed his opposition to the Balfour Declaration, Jewish immigration, and the Jewish settlement west of the Jordan. However, while addressing his Arab colleagues and leaders of other Arab nations, he also called for greater moderation toward and acceptance of the Jewish presence in the region. Here was a real politician at work — though it made me wonder where Abdullah truly stood.

I was particularly impressed with a booklet titled *Who Am I?* that Abdullah had written for schoolchildren. In it were sections on Islam and its basic tenets; early and modern history of the Arab people and their leaders; and a survey of modern disciplines including zoology, botany, astronomy, and medicine, along with information on Arabs who had made a contribution in those fields. Written in simple language, the book distilled the basic values and knowledge he wished to impart to Transjordanian youth.

When I returned the box to Abdullah, urging that the material be placed in the library, he shook his head. "No, it's not for public consumption. They will see it when the time is right." That was the last I saw of the ruler's personal writings.

As much as Abdullah liked the library, he also knew, as I did, that other than being a showplace for visitors, the library was rarely used. There were many accomplished people in Amman and around the court — teachers, ministers, government officials, and scholars — but few took advantage of this facility. Because of his failing eyesight, Abdullah himself had little use for the library. The catalogue and the books, organized and elegantly displayed, remained as neglected as they had been before they were put on the shelves. I was left with the feeling that I had built the extravagant project essentially for myself. When I once commented to Abdullah how little the library was used, he responded, half embarrassed and half joking, that the library could use a few thousand people "from the other side," apparently referring to the Jewish community of Palestine whose know-how he hoped to utilize.

His residence now largely rebuilt to his satisfaction, Abdullah had begun to think more about public projects. Deeply committed as he was to raising the level of education and standard of living of his people, he had moved to improve various facilities in Transjordan. The development of a vocational school for boys, a secondary school for girls, and a secondary school for future officers of the Arab Legion were among the projects already under way. He then turned his attention to his next dream — creating a network of medical facilities available to all.

When I first came to Amman I discovered that many of its citizens had never seen a doctor. Instead they would seek the help of a healer when they were sick, or use homemade medications concocted by women in the neighborhood. Crushed aromatic plants and the protective power of magical charms were believed to be the most effective ways of dealing with disease. The more educated used the services of a hospital run by an Italian organization and funded by the Mussolini regime. Others went to a number of small clinics supported by Christian organizations and run by missionaries. The upper crust of Amman society sought medical care at Jewish medical facilities in Palestine.

When it was time to begin planning the medical network, Abdullah knew exactly where to look. He thought of Hadassah Hospital in Jerusalem, considered the most advanced in the Middle East. Established by an American woman named Henrietta Szold in 1912, it grew into a system of facilities scattered throughout the country, the center being located on Mount Scopus in Jerusalem. The Hadassah Hospital employed the services of many physicians and scientists who had fled Nazi persecution.

Abdullah had once met the director of the hospital, Dr. Chaim Yasky, when he visited a cousin hospitalized there. Dr. Yasky received Abdullah and took him on an extensive tour of the hospital. So impressed was Abdullah that when the time came to find a medical consultant, Yasky was his choice.

A special luncheon was organized at the Raghdan Palace in honor of Yasky and two colleagues. I was invited along to act as interpreter. The table was set with white linen and beautiful silver dishes, and a menu of stuffed vegetables, lamb, sweets, and fruit was served. Unfortunately, Abdullah's conversation that day did not inspire the appetite. Indeed he told a story so gory I could hardly concentrate on the translation. But translate it I did:

A young sheikh, a son of the nobility known for his courage and chivalry, was badly injured in the leg. The oldest and most experienced healer was called in. He slowly walked to the tent, washed his hands and feet, circled the patient a few times, then knelt facing Mecca and prayed. He began chanting in a whisper, but his voice grew louder and louder, until it could be heard throughout the encampment, drowning out the agonizing cries of the wounded youth.

The healer then chopped some aromatic herbs and ground them into powder, boiled some butter, and mixed it with the powder until it became a smooth paste. He smeared the paste on the wound, then took a can out of his pocket. When he opened the can an army of large black ants crawled out. He put the ants on the wound and they got to work. The ants pulled and stretched the edges of the patient's skin toward the middle of the wound until it was closed.

The patient, meanwhile, was sweating and his face was turning blue. Only his heavy breathing indicated that he was still alive. The ants were brushed away with a rag and the wound covered. The young man was placed between two kneeling camels to warm his body.

The boy's father wanted the healer to take some meat, goat cheese, and rice for his family as payment, but he refused. All he would take was some flatbread and a few sugar cubes. He mounted the camel and disappeared. Fully recovered, the young man rejoined his raiding party within a few days.

Dr. Yasky found the story amusing and commented

that if Abdullah described his medical observations in writing, he would undoubtedly get a medical degree from the Hebrew University. A good laugh on the part of all the listeners opened the way to more serious business.

Abdullah outlined the plan he had in mind, and offered Yasky the job of consultant to the project. A talented architect named Hoffmann, who had done a great deal of work for the mandate government in Palestine, was recommended to do the building plans. The British government in Transjordan and the high commissioner in Jerusalem had promised to provide funds. The hospital was ready to be launched.

The Department of Public Works (known by citizens as the "department for delay") had the authority to approve, reject, or modify a government project. True to form, its officials began to raise objections as soon as the foundations were dug and ready to be laid. The first issue involved the standard by which the consistency of the cement was to be measured. They insisted the British standard be used, despite the fact that the British themselves used the less costly cements based on Belgian and French standards. Cement samples were sent to laboratories in Tel Aviv, Damascus, and Beirut, which caused long delays. By the time approval was obtained, months had gone by and the cost of cement and steel skyrocketed. The contractor was no longer able to proceed. Though he had already invested a large sum of money digging the foundations, he had to cut his losses and abandon the project. In the end, plans for the central hospital were shelved and only one small clinic in Amman was ever completed. The gaping foundation holes remained untouched.

I heard of Dr. Yasky again in connection with a tragic event that took place in Jerusalem in April 1948, a few weeks before the cessation of the British mandate in Palestine. War between the Arabs and Jews was already raging in Jerusalem. A convoy of ambulances and buses, guarded by armored cars, tried to reach Mount Scopus, where the Hadassah Hospital and the Hebrew University were located. The passengers were mainly physicians, nurses, professors, students, and hospital workers. When the convoy passed the Arab quarter of Sheikh Jarrah, a mine exploded and the whole convoy was engulfed in heavy gunfire. A British colonel attempted to intervene and stop the fire, but to no avail. He called the British headquarters, located only a mile away, and asked for permission to use heavy artillery to disperse the attackers. Permission was denied. When reinforcements finally reached the area several hours later, the vehicles had been destroyed by firebombs. Seventy-eight people, among them world-renowned scientists who had fled Nazi Germany, were killed. One of the dead was Dr. Yasky.

8

The Doors to the Harem

IT TOOK ONLY A FEW MONTHS after our arrival for our presence at the court to seem almost routine. People stopped staring and accepted us as part of the scenery. I was able to come and go as I pleased. No doors were barred to me, with one exception — those to the women's harem.

Hidden away behind locked doors, the women remained a mystery. Not only were they hidden from view, they were not to be mentioned in conversation. To ensure there be no misunderstanding, we were assigned a special guide on matters of conduct concerning women in the court. The man was a hajji, a clergyman of high standing who had acquired his status from having made a pilgrimage to Mecca. His job was to supervise our activities and to make sure we didn't linger in any area from which the women's windows could be observed. Even strolling behind the harem quarters was to be avoided. If one of my men approached an area designated as out-of-bounds, a guard would appear as if from nowhere and inform the trespasser, sometimes politely but more often gruffly, that "Sayidna doesn't want men to be walking near his women's home." The women's presence was nonetheless very much felt.

Since the Great Hall was located between the two women's quarters, we often overheard their conversation, laughter, and singing while we were working on the parquet floor. We also had the feeling that they were watching us. When one of us, whether inadvertently or deliberately, lifted his eyes toward the stairway or the balconies, he would occasionally catch a glimpse of a passing shadow. Our curiosity grew.

In the evening, when all the workers had left the hall, the women would leave their harem and inspect the floor. They would assess the progress and walk around, confident no one was watching. One evening three of my youngest workers mustered their courage, or their stupidity, and at the end of the day, instead of leaving with the rest of us, hid behind a pillar in the hall and waited until the women came out.

Two of Abdullah's daughters and their maid walked in unveiled, clad in light summer dresses. The moment they saw the men they fled in horror. When I heard the men's story, I was shocked at the men's audacity. A violation of this nature could have severe consequences. Termination of the contract and expulsion would have been the most benign result. Physical punishment such as flogging or imprisonment were possible under such circumstances. We hoped that the women would remain silent; their behavior would have been even more severely punished. Fortunately for us, they kept the incident secret.

As a devout Muslim, Abdullah enforced the strictest Islamic rules within the women's quarters. To guarantee total compliance, each woman was assigned a eunuch to oversee her actions. While day-to-day discipline was maintained by the chief eunuch, Aam Shakif, the emir dealt personally with the most serious transgressions, and applied tough punitive measures. There were rumors circulating about the severity of his floggings, though it was hard to tell whether they were based on fact or yet another product of the myth-making so prevalent at court. One could not ignore, however, the cries and pleas for mercy that could sometimes be heard coming from the inner rooms of the harem.

Islamic law permitted a man four wives and an unlimited number of concubines. Sharifa Misbah, Abdullah's first wife, also his cousin, was promised to Abdullah at birth as part of an agreement between their two families. This union gave her an important position, with the title Great Emira. She gave birth to two children, a daughter named Haya and a son named Talal, who as the eldest male was next in line to the throne of Transjordan.

While Abdullah's first marriage was dictated by tradition and extended-family considerations, his marriage to the Minor Emira was the result of free choice. She was said to be of Turkish-Tartar origins. Abdullah met her during a stay in Istanbul and was attracted by her good looks, vivaciousness, and intelligence.

The Great Emira did not take kindly to Abdullah's choice of a second wife. She had expected Abdullah to select a woman of equal or nearly equal status, as would befit a man who heeds family tradition. She therefore considered his marriage to a commoner an insult to her honor and the honor of her children. It was said at court that since his second marriage she had lost respect for Abdullah and was estranged from him.

The two wives lived in separate wings of the harem, each with its own entrance, kitchen, drivers, servants, and eunuchs. The women could not visit each other without permission from Abdullah, and he preferred to keep his two wives apart. Only the aroma of cooked food coming from their kitchens and the noise of their phonographs intermingled in the hallways.

The two wings of the harem were filled with women from all walks of life. Besides Abdullah's wives and children, there were relatives and guests who came to stay temporarily or permanently. In addition, dozens of servants and eunuchs lived in or around the harem. Chauffeurs, cooks, and other male servants lived on a separate floor and were escorted into the harem by the eunuchs. All conversation between male employees and the women was mediated by the eunuchs.

The wives, daughters, and assorted female relatives who lived in the segregation of the harem were often bored. None had ever accompanied Abdullah on his trips, and few had received a formal education. Abdullah's wives and daughters could read and write Arabic, but the others were illiterate. Their time was occupied by concerns over wardrobe, cosmetics, and jewelry, though men other than family members never caught a glimpse of any of this finery, and it was all for display among themselves.

Aam Shakif was to become our link to the harem. Shakif was a eunuch who had served in the harem of Abdullah's father, Hussein. He was said to be seventy years old, though no one really knew his age. He was tall and well built, with a smooth, beardless face. While other eunuchs were considered subhuman and subjected to abuse, humiliation, and mockery, Shakif was treated with great respect at court. His elevated status was due not only to his authority over and familiarity with matters concerning the women but also to the widespread belief that he possessed magical powers. He was reputed to have the ability to communicate with spirits and to minimize the impact of curses, and was a master of rituals designed to drive away the evil eye. Shakif was particularly alert to the danger of a whistling sound, lest the sound awaken dormant evil spirits. If Shakif heard my men hum or whistle a tune, he would demand they stop immediately.

The only person who dared to play havoc with Shakif's magic was Mohammed Zubati, the court manager. For no apparent reason other than to taunt Shakif, Zubati would make sharp whistling sounds that inevitably provoked great fear among the harem. Shakif and the women would run and huddle in a dark corner, hoping that the evil spirits would overlook them.

Shakif used to spend many idle hours with us, holding forth on a wide range of topics. To heighten the mystery and to whet our curiosity, he would throw in an occasional random comment about the harem. It was always difficult to tell fact from fiction in Shakif's discourse, but we eagerly awaited his company, for he was our only contact with the subject of women during the long weeks away from our families. (The women on the other side of the harem doors were apparently equally interested in the bits of fact and fantasy he brought back about the strange *yahud* working just outside those doors.) Even such isolated comments, however, were a violation. All talk about women, and particularly the emir's wives and daughters, was strictly forbidden.

This veil of secrecy was soon to be lifted. My entrance into the harem occurred as the result of the accident in the wing belonging to the Minor Emira. A broken pipe caused gallons of water to gush onto the emir's beautiful rugs on the lower level. The emir asked me to accompany Shakif to the Minor Emira's quarters and also granted permission for two of my workers to come along.

Shakif escorted us to the second floor by way of a marble stairway. When we reached the locked doors of the residence, Shakif banged on the door and shouted "*tarik!*" (make way!) at the top of his lungs. This was a signal for the women to go into hiding. Shakif waited until all the scurrying sounds had ceased and he was finally satisfied that the women were out of sight, then he opened the door. There was total silence in the front hall, but we could hear the women whispering and giggling behind closed doors in adjoining rooms. They were probably peeking out of keyholes, trying to witness this most unusual event.

The palace plumbing required frequent repairs and further incursions into the harem. At first Shakif would lead the way, sending the women into hiding. As repairs continued, visits had to be made without the explicit approval of the emir, and in time even Shakif's door-banging became more sporadic and his surveillance over us less consistent.

One day the Minor Emira appeared in person. Her face was veiled and a black dress covered her body down to her ankles. She greeted me formally and thanked me for a job well done. Gradually the women stopped scurrying away when we arrived. The emira's daughters would sometimes walk by, also fully veiled, and utter a quick greeting. They eventually dropped their veils and even stopped by for a brief chat.

Such contacts, seemingly insignificant by Western standards, were a revolutionary departure from court protocol and tradition. Nonetheless, it was possible for the emir to look the other way when it came to his second wife, as she was not a Hashemite and not of royal blood. Having bent the rules a bit when he married her, he may have found it easier to be less stringent with her. But the utmost respect that was due his first wife, a descendant of the prophet Mohammed, required stricter adherence to the Koranic code. It took several years — and severe decay of the plumbing system in her wing — before we were allowed to set foot in the holiest of holies, the harem of the Great Emira.

Women could leave the harem only with the express permission of the emir. On occasion one would see women strolling in the orchards. They were veiled and escorted by eunuchs, who walked on either side of their path to prevent men from approaching. At other times the women could be seen riding in one of the royal cars, with curtains and shades drawn tight.

In the years that followed, the rules became more relaxed and it became more acceptable for the women to leave their residence. During the Second World War, some were even allowed to cross into Palestine to go shopping. They began to be seen in stores in Tel Aviv and Jerusalem buying clothes, jewelry, and cosmetics. They even engaged in petty smuggling of goods across the border, making a little extra money for themselves. Trips across the border had to be short, however, because the women were forbidden to spend the night away from the harem in Amman.

I remember an event involving the Minor Emira's daughters that occurred during one of their trips. On their way back to Amman their car had broken down, and their curfew was fast approaching. I happened to be in Abdullah's office when he got the call informing him of this, and suggested that the daughters spend the night at my home in Jerusalem under the supervision of my wife. I vouched for their safety and well-being. He would not hear of it. He seemed so preoccupied and enraged that he hardly paid attention to my suggestion. He dispatched another car to Palestine to bring the women back home. They were in their own beds in the harem before midnight. Such adventures would never have come to pass in the house of Sharifa Misbah, the Great Emira, who adhered to the strictest rules of Islam and raised her daughter accordingly.

I often wondered whether the women knew that another life existed only two hours away on the other side of the Jordan. Those who traveled to Tel Aviv and Jerusalem must have seen women moving about freely, with bare faces, arms, and legs, mingling with men without a trace of self-consciousness. Did they resent their status? Did they dream of a life of greater freedom and self fulfillment? The daughters of the Minor Emira were not much older than my own daughter, who was actively engaged in educational and social pursuits, and who had dreams about a career of her own, world travel, and exploring new horizons. It appeared, however, that the women of the harem never questioned the rules. The hierarchies established and the routines followed were believed to follow the will of Allah. Everyone's fate was determined at the beginning of time and not subject to change by man. Some were destined for happiness and comfort, others to suffer at the hands of the more fortunate. Freedom of choice was alien to all of them.

There was one woman in the harem, however, who had not accepted the inevitability of the misery to which she had been born. She was Nahada, the White Morning Star.

9

Nahada, the White Morning Star

WHEN ABDULLAH'S SECOND WIFE, the Minor Emira, gave birth to their son Naif, she received a special gift from her father-in-law, Hussein, grand sharif of the Hejaz. He sent her the best slave in his harem. This woman had a strong, agile body, boundless physical endurance, and a pleasing manner. With her came several children, the youngest of whom was a girl with velvety black skin and dark, sparkling eyes.

The woman and her children settled in the Minor Emira's household, and soon became a welcome addition to the staff. They worked quietly and efficiently, seeking to anticipate the needs of their mistress and her guests. The young daughter, always at her mother's side, was also blessed with boundless energy, a cheerful disposition, and contagious laughter, which enlivened the dullness of the harem. When she grew older, she was assigned to the Minor Emira's daughter, Emira Makhbula, to be both servant and playmate.

Abdullah welcomed the laughter and good humor that the new arrivals brought with them, and enjoyed watching mother and daughter carrying out their daily chores. As a reward for their hard work, Abdullah ordered that they be given better food and clothing, benefits never before afforded to servants in the harem. He further granted the nameless girl special recognition by naming her. He called her Nahada — the White Morning Star.

Scores of legends grew up around Nahada's rise from slavery to eminence, most of them characterized by fantasy and exaggeration. No one really knew the whole story, but one of the versions passed down to me through Makhbula sounded more credible than the others.

It was said that Nahada had once broken some cardinal rule, serious enough to be brought to Abdullah's attention. The punishment called for was flogging at the emir's own hands. Unlike other women, who would cry and beg for mercy, Nahada approached the emir with a smile, ready to accept her punishment. Enraged by her apparent defiance, the emir hit her severely, and the less she protested the harder he flogged her. Nahada still would not utter a word nor shed a tear. When the emir finally gave up, Nahada kneeled and passionately kissed the palm of his hand. It was said that the kiss cast a magic spell on Abdullah and set into motion events that neither the emir nor the young girl could have ever predicted.

Abdullah became enthralled by Nahada. First he began to relieve her of her chores, and then he gave her her freedom, after which she lived as an equal among the other women in the harem. Before long, he established a separate residence for her and her mother not far from the palace. In spite of ill feelings on the part of his wives and children, Abdullah made no effort to curtail his frequent visits to her residence.

Abdullah married Nahada a few months later. People in government offices, at the court, and in the marketplace whispered disapprovingly about this marriage, but no one expressed dismay openly except for Abdullah's older son, Talal, whose anger and humiliation were said to have caused a rift between father and son that would never be bridged.

The animosity and jealousy directed at Nahada were intense. She was shunned by Amman society and was often referred to as *el-abdi*, the black slave. Unfazed, confident of Abdullah's growing devotion, Nahada remained calm and aloof. Her deportment conveyed power and majesty. A smile of satisfaction would appear on her face when she thought about her triumph over the queens of the harem who had fallen out of favor with their master.

Within a year Abdullah decided to build a special palace for his young bride. Although his coffers were almost depleted as a result of the extensive renovations in the main palace, he resolved to go ahead with the building. The funds were drawn from three sources: the court's operating budget, Nahada's own purse — consisting of savings she and her brothers had accumulated from gifts and special allowances — and funds contributed by the Department of Public Works. The new residence was built on a hill, overlooking the city on one side and the emir's palace on the other. To obtain the land, a number of lots and private homes had to be purchased or confiscated, then demolished.

The municipality of Amman paved the road from the main palace to Nahada's house. The Department of Public Works was responsible for building the external structure. The woodwork, electrical wiring, plumbing, and interior furnishing were all turned over to me. An agreement was made in Nahada's presence that all decisions be reached only with her full participation and consent. Though such a stipulation was common among clients in my own country, it was an astonishing concession to a woman in Amman in the late 1930s.

Nahada was surprisingly knowledgeable about the latest innovations in home design. She scoured books and magazines and was sure about what she wanted. She made no compromises with economic reality, because her main goal, as she expressed it, was to make the emir as comfortable as possible when he came to visit. She achieved her purpose. The house that was built contained the latest modern conveniences: a central heating system, electrically equipped kitchen, venetian blinds, walk-in closets, and sanitary bathrooms. Some of these features were absent even in the monarch's own residence.

The interior was done in Middle Eastern style, the floors covered with a variety of Persian rugs, the windows dressed in bright silk, and the upholstered furniture luxurious and comfortable. A profusion of hand-embroidered cushions added extra color and warmth. Western-style conveniences blended with local touches and gave everything an air of romantic informality. Abdullah named it the White Palace, secretly enjoying the fact that it belonged to the black beauty he had found at his harem.

Abdullah made the White Palace his second home and kept some of his best clothing there, as well as official government papers. I heard people around the court grumble that Abdullah was neglecting his other wives and that he was skipping his obligatory morning visits to the households of the Great and Minor Emiras. At one point I took the liberty of broaching the subject of his absence from the harem. He was not offended. "It's all your fault," he said to me. "You are the one who created this haven for me. So what do you expect?"

When the Second World War broke out, the price of materials skyrocketed, and builders were unable to fulfill their contracts without also raising their prices. It was generally accepted that the client would assume some of the burden of the increased cost. Abdullah had been bewildered when I did not ask for an adjustment. We were nearing the completion of Nahada's house when the emir approached me and asked why. He was already accustomed to some of my strange behavior regarding business practices, but this was truly out of the realm of his experience. I explained that the increases did not affect us because the large down payment I received when I began the work had enabled me to purchase all the necessary materials before the price escalation. He understood my words but failed to understand my attitude. When he returned to the court, he shared his puzzlement with others, who then repeated the story to still others. I remained an enigma until my last day there.

My work at the White Palace brought me into daily contact with Abdullah and Nahada. Both came to trust me and to treat me as a friend. Nahada expressed a wish to get to know my family. This was not difficult to arrange, since she traveled to Jerusalem quite frequently. My wife and I had the opportunity to entertain her in our home during one of those trips. As she entered the house, she looked around and exclaimed, without a shred of embarrassment, "From what I hear, Jews have untidy homes, but yours is neat and sparkling." To which my wife responded quickly,

"And from what I hear, the king's palaces are poorly kept, yet your house is perfectly clean." It was true that Nahada's home was exceptionally orderly. She employed her own servants, who were constantly on the alert to detect any deviation from perfection. And she didn't mind pitching in and joining the servants, as she enjoyed this type of work and was expert at it.

A few years after the completion of her palace in Amman, Nahada achieved another coup: a second home in Abdullah's winter compound in Shuneh, located in the Jordan Valley to the south of Amman. Although Abdullah normally spent the winter months in a tent village, he was thinking of building a modern complex in Shuneh, which was to include a new private residence, ceremonial halls, apartments for his personal guards, garages, stables, gardens — and most important, a mosque. We worked on the plan together and decided to begin with the construction of the royal residence. After extensive planning, and after the foundations had been laid, the plan was changed. Abdullah decided to postpone work on his own palace and proceed instead with plans for a winter palace for Nahada, to be built near his.

Nahada's winter house turned out to be a magnificent edifice, designed and built entirely by Jewish hands, from the architectural plans to the furniture and appliances. A garden, irrigated by a specially dug canal from the Jordan River, transformed the barren desert around Nahada's house into an oasis of blazing colors. The winter palace in Shuneh and the White Palace in Amman were registered in Nahada's name. She thus became the only one of Abdullah's wives to accompany him to Shuneh in winter, to live independently away from the harem, and to own real estate.

Abdullah's passion for Nahada knew no bounds — nor did Nahada's appetite for power and possessions. She was not satisfied with the two palaces alone. Her heart yearned for green pastures and wide spaces. It took no more than an expression of her whim for Abdullah to turn over to her various pieces of fertile land in the Jordan Valley. Fruits and vegetables grown on this land were sold in the markets of Transjordan and Palestine, and turned a handsome profit.

I found working with Nahada surprisingly easy. She was creative, imaginative, and flexible, but I often wondered whether her charm was self-serving and manipulative or the product of an unencumbered soul that knew the meaning of joy. Was she driven by a childlike naiveté, I wondered, or by power, as was so common among Abdullah's favorites?

And what about Abdullah? I wondered why he yielded so easily to her outrageous whims, and why he permitted her an unprecedented leeway that ended in the greatest coup of all.

When Abdullah was made emir of Transjordan in 1921, the British financed the building of a Diwan on a site facing the old Roman theater in Amman. The Diwan was to serve as the seat of government and Abdullah's official headquarters. Among its frequent visitors were the officials of the British mandate, officers of the Arab Legion, and a host of consultants, as well as farmers and merchants who came seeking justice. There Abdullah would sit, listening patiently, arbitrating conflicts and passing judgments.

Abdullah was thinking of renovating the Diwan and turning it into a majestic building befitting the seat of government. However, Nahada had plans of her own for that piece of real estate. Abdullah didn't bat an eyelash when she made her wish known to him — and to everyone's dumb-founded surprise, he agreed to pass the ownership of the property to her. He ordered the appropriate officials to gather and executed the transfer of the deed to his beloved wife. His hand didn't tremble when he signed the papers. He apparently greatly enjoyed seeing the faces of the officials all gaping at him in horror. The deal was finalized when Nahada dipped her thumb in ink and pressed it on the document. She had become the owner of one of the most valuable pieces of land in Amman, and a revered national site.

With the population of Amman growing, housing construction expanding, and the price of real estate escalating, Nahada realized that the value of the Diwan had peaked and that it was a good time to sell. She approached the owners of the Philadelphia Hotel, which was adjacent to the Diwan, confident that the owners of the only luxury hotel in town would be more than willing to purchase her property.

The hotel owners responded to the offer with a show of indifference, though they must have known they had struck gold. Demand for hotel rooms was enormous, and they were anxious to expand. Never in their wildest dreams would they have believed that the land of the Diwan would be for sale. They agreed to pay a hefty sum, and Nahada agreed to close the deal quickly — before the details leaked out to the British administration and local officials. According to the contract, Abdullah had to vacate the building within three months. The Department of Public Works had no alternative but to build a new facility, adding an extension to the palace to serve as a new Diwan. Had the department bought the Diwan back from Nahada and used it for its original purpose, a great deal of public money would have been saved.

This episode infuriated British officials, since it was their government that shouldered the burden of the expense. Talal, Abdullah's eldest son, was also enraged. Fanciful stories and rumors spread among the general population. As often happened when events were beyond their comprehension, the people of Amman sought an explanation in the powers of magic — in this case a talisman that Nahada was believed to have secretly purchased from a Jewish shaman. But even those who bristled at her financial acumen could not have guessed at her wealth. She was the owner of substantial real estate assets and had holdings in various private companies, including the Transjordan-Iraq Carrier Company. After Abdullah's death it was discovered that many of his personal properties had been signed over to Nahada.

I often wondered about Abdullah's unconditional devotion to his third wife. How could a man so intelligent, so proud of his ancestry, so discerning and wise, give away so much of what was entrusted to him? The answer lay in the depths of a soul known to no one, possibly hidden even from himself. It was more than simply an aging man indulging a vibrant young woman.

There were other court favorites who with the full awareness of the king got away with outrageous actions. In fact, he felt a particular attraction to people who were not afraid of him. Although he demanded complete obedience, he respected those who stood up to him and who did not flinch at his authority. Perhaps for this reason he had a special affinity for scoundrels, and for those with the nerve to live by their own rules. He had more than a bit of the rascal in him and liked doing the outrageous and then watching others gape. But above all, Abdullah was a man of the desert who loved freedom and limitless expanse. He was bored by the trivia of the harem and the intrigues of the court. Nahada, however, was of a different world. She was a creature of the desert he loved, a daughter of the wild.

10

The Rise of Mohammed Zubati

EVEN ABDULLAH'S CLOSEST FRIENDS could not fathom the mystery behind the rapid rise of Mohammed Zubati. He did not succeed by virtue of a glorious ancestry, as he had none. Like Nahada, he was totally illiterate and untutored in the ways of the world, but able to rise from rags to riches and to become the powerful head of the court. The legend of his rise paralleled her own. As with Nahada, Mohammed's power was said to derive from a secret charm he had once acquired from an old Jewish sage in Jerusalem and wore under his clothes at all times. The actual reason for his rise to power may have been less magical, yet was equally implausible.

He was believed to have come to Amman from one of the desert Bedouin tribes, though no one knew for sure. Mohammed himself was uncertain about his origins; he did not know his father's name, nor did he remember his mother. He was a man without a past. Abdullah used to refer to him as "a chip off the devil himself" while musing over the antics of this young man.

When Mohammed was first seen around the royal stables, he was a somber and emaciated boy of about fifteen.

He used to lend a hand to the grooms, eat scraps of leftover food, and sleep in a corner of the stable. No one asked his name or paid much attention to this dark-skinned, dark-eyed waif. A popular tale has it that once when Abdullah was walking by the stables he heard piercing cries from within. When he entered the stable he saw a young man being beaten by one of the stablehands. The young man stopped crying when he saw the emir, but his eyes were begging for help, his fists clenched in anger.

In the spirit of tribal tradition, Abdullah ordered Mohammed Azabali, head of court at the time, to take the boy to the servants' quarters in the main palace, feed him, give him new clothes, and assign him a place among the palace guards. Little did Azabali know that this young man would one day replace him.

Zubati adapted quickly to his new surroundings. His sharp eyes missed nothing and his quick mind was always on alert. He soon grasped the inner workings of the power structure at court and identified potential friends and foes. He made sure to perform odd jobs and small favors for those whose goodwill he sought, but he did not hesitate to shun those he deemed useless. He knew when to yield and when to push. His first moves were small and measured. He spent time at the stables, observing the action, offering a hand, and making minor helpful suggestions. Then gradually he became bolder, and when no one questioned his authority, his suggestions turned into commands.

He climbed up the next step of the power ladder when he was put in charge of the distribution of food to the court, a responsibility that brought him into contact with all members and all corners of the royal household, including the women's quarters. Before long he was everywhere, giving orders, dismissing people, playing friends off against each other, and threatening even the most esteemed of the emir's men.

Abdullah was not oblivious to the behavior of the young rising star, but he did not intervene. Indeed, he tolerated Zubati with a mixture of admiration and indulgence, the way a father would accept the wrongdoings of a favored errant son. So great was the emir's tolerance that he was willing to countenance the overthrow of Mohammed Azabali. The nature of the accusations against Azabali was never clear, but providing proof of guilt was not necessary. Zubati succeeded in convincing Abdullah of Azabali's transgressions and was authorized to dismiss Azabali and confiscate all the possessions he had acquired during his many years of tenure at the court. Words of protest did reach Abdullah, including those from his wives, but he let his young servant have his way.

To confer formal recognition on the new head of court, Abdullah decided to bestow on Mohammed the title of Bey. Affixed to one's name, the title gives its holder special rank and the intimation of an illustrious ancestry. Abdullah also gave Mohammed a maidservant to be his wife. Though not the most beautiful, she was among the most industrious and obedient in the harem. The emir then gave him a house surrounded by a small fruit garden on the outskirts of the palace grounds.

I was once witness to an incident that remained a topic of hushed conversation among members of the court for some time. We were sitting for our midday meal, the usual crowd surrounding the emir at an informal gathering. A messenger bearing a message from the Hejaz succeeded in entering the dining room unannounced. While the delivery of a letter to the monarch while he sat at his meal was most inappropriate, the letter was accepted because it was registered, suggesting that it contained something of importance. Since Abdullah held personal assets in the Hejaz that were being liquidated, he must have guessed at the contents of the envelope. With a mischievous smile on his face, he lifted the envelope to the light, examined it on both sides, then looked around at the people seated at the table, measuring their curiosity. Those who knew him were aware that he was building up to one of his outrageous gestures. Without opening the envelope he declared, "Mohammed, the contents of this envelope are yours."

Mohammed feigned resistance, then took the envelope with a shrug. Slowly and deliberately he examined the envelope, looking at the guests apologetically, as if he were acceding to his ruler's wish only with great reluctance. He tried to appear indifferent as he opened it, ever so slowly, while the guests held their breath. To the amazement of the guests and Abdullah himself, the envelope contained a check for two hundred pounds sterling (about a thousand dollars at that time). The guests were well aware of the emir's growing personal debt, exacerbated by such gestures of generosity, but there was little they could say in the matter.

Abdullah signed the check and, as an afterthought, said to Mohammed, "Don't forget to give some of it to the most deserving servants for the Beiram holiday." Mohammed nodded in agreement and tucked the check into his right pocket. When he left the room, he pulled a few coins out of his pocket and distributed them among his favorite servants.

One day Mohammed was seen on the streets of Amman behind the wheel of a large luxury car, another gift from Abdullah. The car bore the emblem of the court and the coat of arms of the Hashemite dynasty, normally reserved solely for the members of the royal family. Their conspicuous presence on Mohammed's car left no doubt that Mohammed Bey el-Zubati had acquired a place of great honor at the royal court.

As Mohammed gained wealth and power, changes in his attire became visible. His caftans, previously made of homespun cotton, were replaced by colorful silk gowns. With a gold dagger attached to his waist and shiny braids cascading down his shoulders, he carried himself like an Arabian horse, and when he stretched his tall frame, one saw a man who would not be daunted by blowing sand, scorching sun, or the ill wishes of his worst enemies.

Not all of Mohammed's possessions were given to him by his benefactor Abdullah, nor were they all accumulated as the fruits of his labor. He fired staff, confiscated their meager belongings, and made them his own. He withheld payment from people who worked for him and often pocketed the money. More than once, our building projects were delayed because our construction materials had wound up in his backyard — and once they had found their way there, they rarely came back.

Zubati accompanied Abdullah on all his trips, and he always had fascinating stories to tell when he returned. Though these stores were often wild and disconnected, they were always gripping. Some sounded credible; many seemed embellished and exaggerated. When a look of doubt appeared on the faces of his listeners, Mohammed would hasten to give credence to his tale by adding "by the life of Sayidna" to it. Perhaps uneasy about swearing away his benefactor's life when he knew that he was lying, he would often undo his oath by whispering under his breath, "May God prolong his life." That little whispered phrase revealed the difference between fact and fiction.

Zubati's manipulations stopped short of hurting the emir. He was a loyal servant, and never wavered in his allegiance to the man responsible for his well-being. Perhaps it was this dogged devotion that made Abdullah trust the man. Unlike others who showered Abdullah with empty flattery, Mohammed's words of praise conveyed true respect and adoration. He was the son Abdullah wanted — strong and fearless, cunning and ambitious and, above all, fiercely loyal.

11

The King's Sons

ABDULLAH'S TWO SONS, Talal and Naif, were as different from each other as the plains of the Hejaz were from the gentle slopes of Mount Hermon. Where Talal was morose, hot-tempered, and stubborn, Naif was soft-spoken, complacent, and amiable.

Emir Talal, the crown prince, was born in the Hejaz in 1912, two years after the birth of Abdullah's first daughter, Haya. Great affection existed between the young boy and his grandfather Hussein, but the relationship between Talal and his father was fraught with difficulty almost from the start. Unlike Abdullah, who was buoyant and outgoing, Talal disliked effusive flattery and the vagaries of subtle communication. The conflicts between Talal and his father were reminiscent of the disagreements between Abdullah and his own contentious father, but they were far more intense and had far more severe consequences.

It was said at court that Talal had ingested anger toward his father through his mother's milk. Ever mindful of her honorable lineage, the Great Emira guarded the dignity of her ancestry with quiet fierceness. This dignity suffered a severe blow when Abdullah took a Turkish woman as his second wife. It was not the addition of a second wife that so angered the Great Emira — that was to be expected, and was sanctioned by the Koran. It was the low social station from which the Minor Emira came that made the Great Emira and her children feel dishonored.

Talal was a sensitive boy who felt his mother's shame, and in time came to live her pain. He grew up in the somber atmosphere of his mother's household, so different from the relaxed and informal climate of the Minor Emira's. His mother's resentment became his own. His anger turned into rebellion as his rancor grew stronger.

To ensure the necessary preparation for Talal's succession to the throne, Abdullah sent him to England to learn the language, culture, and customs of the people with whom he would probably share the sovereignty of Transjordan. Talal enrolled at Sandhurst, the prestigious military academy also attended by other members of the Hashemite family. For Abdullah, Talal's years at Sandhurst were a time of relative relief. For Talal, they were years of hard work during which he acquired many of the skills necessary for his future role as monarch. Familiarity with the British, however, did not increase his admiration for the people who exercised so much control over his father and his country. He was acutely aware of their less-than-subtle disrespect for his father, and angry about Abdullah's readiness to acquiesce to such humiliation.

When Talal returned home from England, he discovered that most of the duties he had expected to assume had already been assigned, mostly to Mohammed Zubati. He felt that Zubati had stolen his birthright, an impression soon confirmed by fact. Witnessing Zubati's manipulations, and his father's unqualified confidence in the man, Talal tried to persuade his father to get rid of Zubati. Abdullah casually rejected such an idea, but Zubati viewed it as a real threat and was determined to squash this new rival. He repeatedly provoked Talal, denying him his allowance and treating him with scorn. One day the two got into a bitter argument. Talal reportedly lost control and assaulted Zubati. Zubati had achieved his goal.

That incident was only one of several altercations between Talal and other members of the court. The details of such explosions were never discussed openly, but it was rumored that Talal's behavior was caused by mental illness. Later it was diagnosed as schizophrenia. At the time, however, Abdullah perceived his son's behavior as willful belligerence and sent him to Iraq to live with his cousin King Ghazi.

When I first arrived at the palace in 1937, Talal was still in exile. I heard about the relationship between Abdullah and his son from people close to the emir. I also heard that Nuri Said, prime minister of Iraq and a close friend of Abdullah's, had intervened on Talal's behalf and succeeded in achieving a truce between father and son. Talal returned home from Iraq and was given a post in the Arab Legion, though at a salary barely sufficient to feed his family.

Soon after Talal's return to Amman, I was advised by my friends to stay out of his way. He was given to unpredictable fits of anger, they said, and was a true antagonist toward Jews and Zionism. But Abdullah told me that his son had seen my work and wanted to meet me to discuss renovations in his own house. He warned me, however, that Talal was moody and unpredictably abusive, and hoped that I would not take his erratic outbursts personally.

I first met Talal at Raghdan Palace, at a time and place set by Abdullah. Talal addressed me in perfect English, somewhat formally. "I hear a great deal about your work here, and I appreciate your achievements," he said, then immediately proceeded to talk about the renovations he had envisioned for his house. As Talal spoke, his ideas became increasingly fanciful and grandiose, and I immediately became aware of his mental instability.

Talal invited me to his home, a rented house he shared with his wife and children. Since it had previously been owned by a Christian, it lacked the separate entrances for males and females required by Muslim tradition. He hired me to build new entrances, and also to provide space-saving devices that might relieve the overcrowding in the house. Talal did not introduce his wife to me; she remained sequestered in another room throughout my visit. I knew that her name was Zein, and that she was his cousin and a descendant of the same distinguished Hashemite ancestry. When I eventually got to know her, I found her to be sensible and quick to grasp things, but I had no clue as to the immense power and supreme intelligence she would ultimately exercise when her husband's accession to the throne was in jeopardy.

I sensed that Talal was keeping me at arm's length. Our conversations were limited to the customary greetings and business matters. One day, however, during one of his less guarded moments, he apologized and said that he could never form a friendship with a Jew, because Arabs and Jews would never find a common language. "Jews are rich, clever, well educated, and highly capable, while Arabs are poor, illiterate, and primitive. Contact between Arabs and Jews would inevitably put Arabs at a disadvantage and should therefore be avoided." He then added, "As far as you are concerned, Mr. Cohen, I want you to know that I have nothing against you as a person." The words sounded familiar. They echoed sentiments expressed toward Jews throughout history.

Though they were blunt words, they were also refreshing, for they stood in sharp contrast to the circuitous, effusive, and often distorted forms of communication employed at the court. As I looked around the apartment, I began to realize that his gruffness may have been only partly rooted in his illness, and that his anger may have had a base in reality. I wondered how he felt about Mohammed Zubati, the interloper, living in a luxurious home and acquiring additional real estate while Talal and his family were living in cramped rented quarters. How could he justify his father's munificence toward strangers while his flesh and blood was barely making ends meet?

During the Second World War the government instituted food rationing, and Talal's family often found its pantry, which was never full to begin with, empty of food. Talal repeatedly approached the government official in charge of rationing and asked for a bag of rice, only to be put off. One day Talal lost his patience, ran home, loaded his gun, and returned to the man's office, threatening to shoot him. He was arrested and sentenced by his father to a lengthy term of confinement. I consequently learned that

Abdullah had issued a royal edict denying Talal's right to the throne — a decree he subsequently rescinded.

Many of Abdullah's friends and associates worked to reverse the sentence and to make peace between father and son, but Abdullah stood firm. Talal was confined to a large tent guarded day and night by armed soldiers of the Arab Legion. An abandoned house located a mile away from the palace was to be converted into a private prison, and I was assigned the job of doing the work — following plans provided by Abdullah himself. Window bars, iron gates, and a barbed wire fence were installed. But the jail was never used, for Abdullah and Talal were able to reach reconciliation at the very last minute.

Reconciliation, however, did not bring accommodation. Father and son continued to differ on many issues. The education of Talal's oldest son, Hussein, was a major source of disagreement. Talal advocated studies in Arabic language and history, Abdullah the study of English and religion. Since Abdullah took it upon himself to see to the boy's education, he determined which schools Hussein would attend and what type of tutors he would have. As a result, Hussein changed schools and tutors several times during his student days.

Personal and temperamental antagonisms were fueled by fundamental ideological conflicts. Talal's strong nationalistic inclinations clashed with Abdullah's search for peaceful coexistence with the British. Talal snubbed his father's friends in the British government, as well as the British commander of the Arab Legion, viewing Abdullah's cordial relations with them as a sign of weakness, a sell-out. He was outraged that the British had appointed Abdullah commander of the air force but then kept secret the number of planes under his command. And he was exasperated that Abdullah's role in the Arab Legion, his country's British-trained army, was limited to awarding medals and attending opening ceremonies. Talal felt his father's humiliation keenly, and was angry with him for accepting it with a smile.

Unlike Abdullah, who knew the limits of his power and achieved his goals through personal diplomacy, Talal advocated a more confrontational approach toward the British and he believed that ensuring his country's future did not necessarily mean cultivating political and familial ties with the Hashemites in Iraq. Fearing that his cousin Abdul Illah, Hashemite regent of Iraq, was seeking annexation of Transjordan to Iraq, Talal advocated developing stronger ties with Syria and Saudi Arabia. These positions were anathema to Abdullah, who advocated unequivocal loyalty to the Hashemite family and remained antagonistic toward the Saudis.

Talal's explosive behavior often reached such proportions that it necessitated hospitalization. His condition fluctuated between states of lucidity, during which he demonstrated great sensitivity and caring for his family, and periods of total madness, during which he perceived the whole universe, including his immediate family, as his enemy. He spent months, sometimes years, in various treatment centers, seeking a cure for his condition. But a cure could not be found. He remained helpless against the ravages of his malady his entire life.

Abdullah never fully understood the nature of his son's illness and at times believed it a result of his own faulty upbringing. As he once said to me, "I have accomplished a lot in my life but I failed badly in bringing up my oldest son."

Unlike his older brother Talal, Naif, who was born in 1914 to the Minor Emira, harbored no ill feelings toward the British or the Jews; he never held grudges nor indulged in controversy. He kept close to his father, sitting with him during his meals and nodding in agreement at his every word.

Concerned over his son's lethargy and lackluster achievements, Abdullah sent Naif to Victoria College in Egypt, where other boys of the royal family were being educated. He hoped that Naif would be stimulated by the scholarly atmosphere of the school and by the example set by his cousins, but, alas, Naif's teachers found him "ineducable" and sent him home. Abdullah took it upon himself to ignite Naif's dormant intellect by showering him with sayings, stories, bits of information, and jokes, all intended to broaden the young man's perspective. Unfortunately, this had little effect.

Naif grew up in the charmed atmosphere of his mother's household, in which life was free of the worry and competitiveness needed to toughen a man's will. In contrast to the grave atmosphere permeating the Great Emira's wing of the palace, Naif's mother's was informal. Children's boisterous voices could often be heard in the halls as they played and chased each other. Naif had many playmates. In addition to his two younger sisters, there were the children of the guests. Most were Turkish relatives, who brought with them some of the liberal ways and Western notions introduced into their country by its new leader, Mustafa Kemal

Atatürk. Also among Naif's playmates were the offspring of servants who worked in the palace, for the Minor Emira did not object to her son's coming into contact with children of lower social standing. Nahada was among Naif's childhood friends. The walls of the Minor Emira's wing, though guarded as closely as those of her rival, were nevertheless more open to the outside world.

In such an environment Naif grew up pampered, dependent, and aimless, but also patient and agreeable. He got along with everybody, including some of the more contentious and difficult people at the court. Much to his father's delight, Naif was on good terms with Mohammed Zubati, and he maintained a friendly relationship with Nahada, who was shunned by other members of the family. As the rift between Talal and Abdullah grew wider, the bond between Abdullah and his younger son grew stronger.

In an attempt to accelerate Naif's development, Abdullah obtained him a high position in the Arab Legion, where he was decorated and treated with great respect. The level of his performance, however, did not improve. He was tolerated by officers of the Legion because of his status and his amiability, but his role was essentially limited to ceremonial duties.

Abdullah made another major effort toward Naif's education by sending him to live with the prime minister of Turkey. Aware of Talal's mental problems, he was thinking of Naif as a possible successor to the Hashemite crown, and he hoped that exposure to the life of the Turkish court would broaden Naif's horizons and prepare him for leadership. Abdullah was thinking of the benefits he had himself derived from the fifteen years he had spent in Turkey at the court of Sultan Abdul Hamid. The experience brought him into contact with the West and introduced him to modern diplomacy. But after a year under the tutelage of the Turkish prime minister, Naif returned home virtually unchanged except for a growing fondness for things Turkish.

Like his father, Naif chose a Turkish woman to be his wife. She was Mihrimah Sultana, a great-granddaughter of the sultan Abdul Aziz. Born in Istanbul and educated in Paris and in Cairo, she was graced with charm, nobility, and a mind of her own. Abdullah rejoiced at this union and was willing to overlook those of her customs he considered improper. She was, for example, a great deal more independent and free-thinking than most other women of her standing, and unlike other women of the court, who hid their faces behind black veils, she used only a light transparent veil to cover half her face.

Abdullah approached me on the matter of building a suitable house for Naif and his bride-to-be. I offered Naif the opportunity to work together, so we might devise plans that would meet his specifications, but whenever I asked for his opinion, he would give me the same answer: "What do I know? Do whatever you think best." Unable to get anywhere with the prince, I asked Abdullah's permission to meet with the fiancée. Abdullah made arrangements for me to go to Cairo to meet her. I went armed with plans and options, and within a few hours the young woman and I were able to work out the necessary details. She proved to be quite knowledgeable and decisive.

Naif's wedding was a major national event, lasting seven days and seven nights. The palace and government buildings were flooded with colorful lights that flickered in the night sky. Some said that the lights could be seen from the rooftops in Jerusalem.

A little of Naif's wife's ambition and energy must have rubbed off on him, for he began to pursue wealth and power more aggressively. The princess discovered that her great-grandfather the Turkish sultan had owned a piece of land hugging both banks of the Jordan River, and that the land had never been passed on to his heirs. The portion of the land that lay in Transjordan was barren and of little value, but the value of the portion located in Palestine was escalating, due to enormous demand from Jewish developers. Convinced that they were the rightful heirs to the land, Naif and his wife initiated legal action against the authorities of the British mandate in Palestine, which proclaimed its guardianship over the property. The litigation preoccupied Naif and his wife for several years and drained them both emotionally and financially. They finally gave up the battle. Naif returned to his position in the Arab Legion, which paid him, like his older brother, a salary barely sufficient to cover basic expenses.

With the help of his resourceful wife, Naif looked for creative new solutions to his financial woes. During the Second World War, Transjordan became the capital of smuggling activity for the entire Middle East. It was not considered a crime and was practiced in the open. Often when I would meet an old acquaintance on the street and ask what he was doing, "doing a bit of smuggling" was the unabashed reply. Even respectable citizens and members of the court, including Prince Naif and his sisters, engaged in black market dealings.

Many branches of the economy were dependent upon smuggling. Gold in the form of coins and bullion, expensive wool and silk clothing, Persian rugs, cigarettes, medications, nylons, spare auto parts, and fountain pens, as well as wheat and other food products, were all smuggled through Transjordan to its neighbors and beyond. Customs police at the major river checkpoints between Transjordan and Palestine would casually watch while the transfer of goods took place in full view only a short distance away. There were two ferries run by local farmers and fishermen between Transjordan and Palestine, serving travelers who wished to avoid inspection, such as people who lacked official documents, escaped convicts, and smugglers. The fee was nominal and the crossing risk-free.

I disapproved of this practice and often had to remind myself that Western notions of national boundaries were foreign to the sons and daughters of the desert nomads. To the Bedouin who lived in the region, there were no clear borders between the territories they crossed to find grazing for their herds. They held loyalty to no state or country, but rather to the heads of their clans and the chiefs of their tribes. It had only been two decades since the new nation called Transjordan had been formally established, in 1921, and the formalities associated with border crossings were still foreign to the soul of the roaming nomads.

Naif went into the smuggling business with uncharacteristic enthusiasm. He did not have to resort to using the ferry up the Jordan River, for his goods were brought in by royal vehicles that were exempt from inspection. His business flourished and money flowed in but, alas, it also flowed out in luxurious hotels, restaurants, and nightclubs in Jerusalem and Tel Aviv.

Naif's good fortune came to an end one day when he was caught red-handed by the British police in Palestine. One story has it that Naif ran into difficulty with his partners, and that they tipped off the Palestine customs police. Naif was stopped when he was about to enter Jerusalem and arrested. When word came from above to release him, he was sent home. News of the incident was hushed.

By this point Abdullah was deeply worried about the future of the Hashemite dynasty. Naif was failing to demonstrate signs of leadership. Abdullah's disappointment became apparent to me during an unusual incident. He was expecting sheikhs from the south who were coming to demand tax reductions. He was not about to give in to this, and asked Naif to accompany him to the tent where he was going to confront them. Naif walked into the tent with his father, but disappeared a few minutes later. Abdullah called out for him to come back, and Naif returned, only to disappear again. Out of patience, and ignoring the fact that his subordinates were witnessing his shame, Abdullah cried out, "You see what I have? I have one son who is out of his mind and another who can't stand by my side for even a few minutes!"

Naif visited my house in Jerusalem on a number of occasions, and used to drop in to my workshop for a chat and a sip of coffee. As usual he was amiable, but he lacked the wit and authority his father commanded. I always pictured him dwarfed by his father's shadow, and never could have imagined that he would be involved in the struggle for the succession to his father's throne.

Abdullah's awareness of his sons' limitations, and his ambivalence about his choice of a successor, became vividly apparent when he approached me on the matter of an official throne for the soon-to-be-independent Hashemite Kingdom of Jordan. This time he showed none of his characteristic decisiveness. One proposal was that the king's throne be built on a platform and that his sons' chairs be situated on a lower level on either side. This plan was rejected because Abdullah didn't want to seat his elder son on his right. Another possibility was to build a wide chair, which could seat two or three people, as necessary. This proposal was also abandoned. He finally ordered that a simple oak chair, upholstered in red velvet, be built on a platform and serve as a provisional throne until a permanent solution might be found. That solution was never found during my tenure at the court. The king sat on a temporary throne in his magnificent palace, unable to determine who should reign after him.

12

The Education of Mohammed Zubati

HAVING CLIMBED TO THE PINNACLE OF SUCCESS, Mohammed Bey el-Zubati would not be satisfied with a humble home, nor with a homely wife who gave him three daughters and no sons. A man of his rank deserved a showplace and a suitable second wife who would be admired by all. He purchased a small stone house and turned over to me the job of converting it into a "grand palace." His notions of a dream house reflected the influence of royal residences he had seen on his trips abroad, embellished by his own imagination.

I found myself entering the web of Mohammed's dreams and getting caught up in the fervor of his ecstasy. For the first time in the course of our relationship, we were on similar wavelengths. We spent many nights poring over blueprints, planning and exploring options. Mohammed spared neither energy nor money trying to turn dream into reality. Once the construction was under way, however, he lost interest and attended to the project only intermittently. I was not surprised, since I had seen him do the same in other instances: he would devote all his energy to attaining an objective only to neglect it once it was secured.

A beautiful home was built for Zubati with all the latest amenities. A chiseled stone facade, marble floors, terraced gardens, silk drapes, and Persian carpets were all coordinated to give the house a feeling of opulence and comfort. Like many other luxurious homes in Amman, however, its major drawback was lack of electrical power. Petroleum stoves and kerosene lamps were still being used for heating and lighting. Nonetheless, Mohammed instructed me to buy him an electric refrigerator. I wondered how a refrigerator was going to work without electricity, but I went along and asked about specifications concerning make, size, and type. Mohammed responded with a shrug. "What difference does it make?" he asked. "Large, small, or even one that doesn't work, so long as everybody knows that Mohammed Bey has a Frigidaire."

I purchased a refrigerator, as well as the other electrical appliances he had asked for, guessing that Mohammed would find a way to activate them. And indeed he did not betray my expectations. He discovered a way to bring electricity into his house.

Pinhas Rutenberg, a Palestinian Jew who was the founder and director of the Palestine Electricity Corporation, channeled electricity to the royal court free of charge as part of a joint venture between Transjordan and the Jewish community in Palestine. Zubati told Rutenberg that the house he was building was part of Abdullah's court complex and that it needed court electricity. Rutenberg saw through the deception but chose to ignore it, and extended the service to Mohammed's household. With the help of Jewish electrical workers, Rutenberg transferred a spare power line to Zubati's house and, for good measure, added a variety of lighting fixtures and cooking appliances at no extra cost.

That was not the only indirect contribution the Jews of Palestine made to the insatiable Zubati. Saplings of fruit trees and flowering shrubs delivered to the royal court by the Agriculture Department of the Jewish Agency as a gift to Abdullah were transferred by Zubati to his own house to adorn the terraces and groves. Neither Abdullah nor the donors were oblivious to Zubati's stratagems, but Abdullah did not seem to mind, and the Jews welcomed the opportunity to establish good relations with the Jordanian ruler's right-hand man. In the end Zubati repaid these favors many times over when he served as liaison between Abdullah and the Jewish leaders of Israel on the eve of the 1948 war. His house was used as a meeting place for Golda Meir and Abdullah in their last-ditch effort to avert the conflict.

Pleased with the progress of the building, Zubati expressed his gratitude to me and my workers in ways that were, for him, highly uncharacteristic: he paid us on time and made his cars and chauffeurs available to us whenever we needed them. He also made arrangements for us to tour some of the most interesting sites in Transjordan. The local Arab laborers, however, received none of his largesse. Every morning, before the workers' arrival, he would set his watch ahead and every evening, before their departure, he would set it back — a devious way of reducing their already meager wages. He rarely paid for overtime; in its place he offered praise and blessings. "God will grant you strength and good health" was often given in lieu of tangible rewards, and when the men asked for money he would reply, "But didn't

I give you Allah's blessings and doesn't that mean more to you than a few brass coins?"

When I first began working for Mohammed, I used to see the workers sitting in front of his house at the end of the day waiting to be paid. Mohammed would get into his car and drive away, leaving the men behind to wait for hours until his return. When he finally came back he would yell at the men for hanging around his house and disturbing the peace. He would promise to pay *"bukra,"* tomorrow. But one *bukra* would turn into another, and then another, often extending for weeks.

This practice used to trouble me greatly, since it stood in such contrast to labor-management relations in the Jewish community in Palestine. The Histadrut, the Jewish Labor Federation in Palestine, was established to ensure fairness in employment and to promote partnerships between workers and employers. I was not particularly fond of organized labor. I preferred to view the employer-employee relationship as personal. My brother Shalom, who was an organizer for the Labor Federation, considered my views a throwback to nineteenth-century benevolent paternalism. He even went so far as to make an abortive attempt to unionize my workers, threatening to call for a strike if I stood in the way. But though I was no great friend to organized labor, I could not tolerate Zubati's mistreatment of laborers. When I saw Zubati's workers squatting at the gate of his house and waiting to collect their wages, I was reminded of a passage from Deuteronomy:

> Thou shalt not oppress a hired servant who is poor
> and needy, whether he be of thy brethren, or of thy

strangers who are in thy land . . . : At his day thou shalt
give him his hire, neither shall the sun go down upon it;
for he is poor, and setteth his heart upon it.

I decided to address this problem head-on and told Mohammed that I would not be able to continue working for
him so long as such inequities existed. I demanded that the
workers be given better conditions and that rules governing
working hours and payment be established and followed.
Mohammed agreed, his usual dauntless bravado retreating.
He understood that I meant every word I said.

Mohammed's thirst for power and riches could not be
quenched. The more he got, the more he wanted. It was
particularly important for him to make his house more
resplendent than the homes of Abdullah's sons; he often
reminded me of this point. While the monarch's sons had
no assets of their own, Zubati managed to acquire valuable
pieces of real estate in various parts of the country and in
neighboring Syria. Naif was living in a relatively modest
house and Talal in cramped rented quarters, but Zubati was
surrounded by riches and comfort in his magnificent home.
Now he could look for a second wife.

Mindful of the scorn with which he was often treated by the
educated elite of Amman, Mohammed Zubati knew that his
growing power and his favor with the emir had not earned
him the unequivocal respect he sought. He concluded that
his life was missing an essential ingredient: an educated
woman of beauty and breeding who would reflect his pres-
tige.

He was determined to choose a woman rather than to

receive one from Abdullah, and he was going to search for the fairest of them all. He did not have to look far. She was a native of Damascus, a center of culture and fashion and known for its sophisticated women, who had come to Amman to live with her widowed mother and work as an English teacher. She was referred to as the *mualmah*, teacher, or the *shami*, the Syrian. I never learned her real name. Zubati first saw her in the Minor Emira's harem, where she was a frequent visitor. She was particularly attractive to him not only because of her good looks but also because she was highly respected among Amman's intelligentsia.

With the assistance of the Minor Emira's daughters he was able to arrange for a number of meetings with the young woman, and the more he saw her the more enchanted he became. She was equally taken by his charm and refused to consider suitors from the upper crust of Amman's families. Even her mother preferred Zubati to the other young men seeking her daughter's companionship. To both mother and daughter Mohammed seemed like the ideal match. He was handsome, rich, and, most important, an intimate of the King. Mohammed Zubati, master of illusion, had succeeded in touching the hearts of both women.

Abdullah disapproved of Zubati's choice and minced no words in expressing his objection. "If you are determined to take another wife, you should rely on me to find you a woman as handsome as a piece of gold," he told him. "You mustn't court a broken vessel from Damascus, a *shami* who will no doubt bring you disgrace. Choose one who is obedient and well respected, and she will make your home a palace." Abdullah was suspicious of all Syrians and believed that behind their polite manners and elegant speech lay harshness and insincerity. He was most intolerant of the flirtatiousness of urban Syrian women and thought them dishonest. I knew Abdullah harbored little affection for the Syrians, with whom he shared an uneasy border and who were ardent antimonarchists, but I also wondered whether Abdullah was having trouble accepting the fact that his protégé was putting his fate into someone else's hands.

Mohammed listened intently and murmured his agreement with his master's admonitions, but he ignored them. His heart and soul were so captivated by the young woman from Damascus that he began to unlock his sealed money chest to buy his beloved and her mother expensive gifts. His coffers, which had been used only to hoard, were now opened wide to provide anything their hearts desired.

The betrothal ceremony, called *ketiba* or "drawing of a marriage agreement," was carried out to the letter of the law. A *ketib*, a person in charge of drafting the betrothal agreement — usually the groom's father or next of kin — asks for the hand of the prospective bride and offers a dowry to the bride's family. Abdullah, who regarded Mohammed's choice with displeasure, nonetheless agreed to serve as *ketib*. He had become accustomed to letting Mohammed have his way. And like an indulgent father, Abdullah not only forgave Mohammed but offered him a gift of five hundred pounds, a princely sum, to help pay for the completion of his house.

The day after the betrothal, Mohammed appeared on the streets of Amman with his long hair cut short, a gesture to please his modern wife. This was the first sacrifice he had ever made for a woman, and also the last. The Amman grapevine hummed with predictions, stories, and jokes. Some gossips likened Mohammed to Samson, who cut his

Mendel Cohen, standing in front of one of the olive-wood cabinets he designed.

King Abdullah, sitting in the courtyard of the Diwan, where he often held conferences with citizens coming to seek his guidance. BETTMANN NEWSPHOTOS

Raghdan Palace, Amman, as it appears today.
JORDANIAN INFORMATION BUREAU, WASHINGTON, D.C.

Hussein ibn Ali, grand sharif of Mecca and king of the Hejaz.
JORDANIAN INFORMATION BUREAU, WASHINGTON, D.C.

Abdullah ibn Hussein.
JORDANIAN INFORMATION BUREAU, WASHINGTON, D.C.

Talal ibn Abdullah, second king of the Hashemite Kingdom of Jordan. JORDANIAN INFORMATION BUREAU, WASHINGTON, D.C.

Hussein ibn Talal, current king of the Hashemite Kingdom of Jordan.
JORDANIAN INFORMATION BUREAU, WASHINGTON, D.C.

King Abdullah and his friend Sir John Bagot Glubb, commander of the Arab Legion, playing chess. ROYAL WAR MUSEUM, LONDON

Mendel Cohen (left) and friends at an outdoor café in Amman, 1937.

Mendel Cohen (third from left) with friends on a trip into the Syrian Desert.

Bedouin tent in the gray-pebbled hamada *of the Syrian Desert.*

Qusar el-Art, one of the citadels in the Syrian Desert.

Nahada's palace under construction.

Mendel Cohen (center) with Jewish and Arab friends, getting ready for an excursion.

Mohammed Zubati, court manager (top row, second from right) and Mr. Azar, court treasurer (top row, third from right), with members of Mendel Cohen's construction crew.

Sholem the miller and his wife Rebecca, 1898, grandparents of Adaia Shumsky. Sholem ran the first mechanized flour mill built outside the walls of Jerusalem's Old City. The mill was destroyed during the 1948 war.

Millstones from Sholem's mill, now adorning a small park where the mill once stood.

King Abdullah and his medical advisor, Dr. Shakrat (wearing fez), at a meeting with Dr. Yasky (third from right), director of the Hadassah Hospital in Jerusalem in 1939. Mendel Cohen is at far right.

Cable car strung across the Valley of Hinnom, used to transport supplies to the Jewish garrison on Mount Zion during the 1948 war. Mendel Cohen was the first to ride the car across the valley.

Mendel Cohen's library in his factory. On the shelves are copies of **The Harash** *(The Artisan), a magazine Cohen founded and edited.*

The Sheikh Hussein crossing point between Israel and Jordan, 1995.

hair to please Delilah and ended by losing his strength and virility. Others insisted that the loss of hair foreshadowed Zubati's loss of power at the court and that he would end up on the street like his predecessor Mohammed Azabali.

Abdullah also viewed the change with displeasure. He believed that a man willing to alter his appearance to please a woman was indeed weak. But, as usual, his annoyance with Zubati faded quickly, or so it seemed.

Abdullah's generous wedding gift was not forthcoming. Shortage of money, which often prevented Abdullah from fulfilling his generous promises, may have been one reason, his feelings about Mohammed's choice of bride, another. Mohammed feared that he was being punished for disregarding his master's advice. Visibly agitated, he approached me one day, asking that I intervene on his behalf and remind the emir of his promise. Normally I avoided running interference for Mohammed, but this time I agreed. The money in question was intended to pay my bill. Abdullah's response surprised me. It was the first time that I heard him complain about his young confidant. "I'm sick and tired of this Mohammed. I can't stand his manipulations and his refusal to listen to my advice. He took this *shami* against my will and should be flogged twenty times. But what can I do if I love him more than my own sons? *Inshalla* [God willing] I will give him the money."

My men and I had worked feverishly to complete the work before the wedding — construction workers, carpenters, painters, and upholsterers all worked together, creating one of the most attractive homes in Amman. Mohammad took his bride on a five-day shopping spree to the most elegant stores in Tel Aviv. Upon his return, feeling proud and confident, he told me with a wink: "From now on she belongs to me and I can do with her as I please. She won't give me trouble because I will hit her with my whip the first time she tries."

Muslim women generally accepted their husbands' decision to wed a second, and sometimes a third, wife, but some adjusted to it better than others. Zubati's first wife did not adjust well. She fell ill the moment she became aware of her husband's growing interest in the Syrian beauty. Mindful of Zubati's lack of concern, Abdullah took it upon himself to find a cure for her malady. Following the advice of his doctors, he found her a house in the village of Suweilah, known for its fresh air and pure water. He provided servants to care for her and made sure that food and medication were delivered to her daily. Mohammed was irked by Abdullah's attention to his first wife's needs. He saw her as a reminder of his early days, when he had to make do with a lowly wife who had once been a servant. He interfered with the delivery of goods to her house by ordering the drivers to engage in other tasks. Shortly before her thirtieth birthday, she died.

Mohammed's second wife and her mother did not fare much better under his roof. As the Arabic proverb has it, *Marrah assal u marrah bassal*, or, one day is honey and the next is onion. The days of honey were soon replaced by a far more bitter reality. First came the confiscation of all reading matter, including books, magazines, and newspapers. Next came a prohibition against the *shami* going out in public without his surveillance. Even access to the verandah, which faced only desert mountains, was forbidden, as were visits by female friends and relatives. She was denied access to the telephone. All incoming calls were directed toward Mohammed, and only those for him were accepted. When Mohammed was out of the house, he would instruct the phone company to hold all calls until his return. Restrictions imposed on the daughter applied to the mother as well; Mohammed believed that purchase of the daughter had included the mother. Within a few months of the marriage, the young wife and her mother were captives in their own home, condemned to roam aimlessly among its many rooms.

Considering women as chattel was common in the Arab world at that time. Many lived under such conditions, accepting them as the unavoidable will of Allah. However, Mohammed's wife and her mother had had different expectations. They had led fairly independent lives prior to the marriage, and had therefore anticipated a greater level of freedom. At first they tried to persuade Mohammed to change his views, but their words only met with punishment. Mohammed often used the whip to keep them in line, and when he was tired he turned the task over to one of the servants, who performed the job with even greater gusto.

Escape was the women's only hope. During one of Mohammed's overnight trips, the women decided to flee north to Syria. In the middle of the night, when all the servants and guards were asleep, the women gathered a few belongings, leaving behind their expensive clothes and jewels, covered their faces with heavy veils, and knocked on the door of a neighbor, who agreed to drive them across the border. The two women held only one passport, for Zubati's wife had had to relinquish her passport soon after she was married. They solved the problem by planning to have the daughter cross first, then give the passport to the driver, who would return it to the mother, so that she could cross.

The daughter crossed the border without difficulty because the border police, out of respect, did not ask her to lift her veil. But the mother, who was the legal holder of the passport, failed to cross. While she was waiting for the driver to return with her passport, one of Zubati's servants discovered that the women had gone. He called his master immediately. The border police were ordered to seize the women. The wife was beyond their reach, but the mother was arrested and returned to Amman.

Unaware of her mother's fate, the daughter arrived at her cousins' home in Damascus and waited. Instead of her mother, two of Mohammed's emissaries appeared at the door, informing her of her mother's arrest. They spared no details describing the punishment inflicted by Mohammed. She knew they were not exaggerating. To spare her mother further suffering, she joined the men and returned to her home in Amman.

A few weeks after the aborted escape I encountered the women under a bizarre set of circumstances. Mohammed had been after me repeatedly to remind Abdullah of the marriage money he had promised. It was not a need for cash that provoked Mohammed's anxiety — he was one of the wealthiest men in Amman — but rather the suspicion that his master was giving him the cold shoulder. I told him that I had done all I could, and that he had no choice but to be patient. After weeks of incessant pursuit, he finally dropped the subject. He had hit upon a new approach.

Late one afternoon Mohammed invited me to join him for supper at his home. Though I wondered what he had in mind, I accepted the invitation. The young *mualmah* and her mother greeted me at the door, a breach of common etiquette signifying an unprecedented freedom in the house. The dining room was brightly lit and the table tastefully set. To my surprise, the women joined us for the meal, another departure from the norm. The women left at the end of the meal. Mohammed and I remained seated at the table and talked. I was accustomed to his fanciful stories, stories that usually carried a latent message, but this time they seemed to lead nowhere. I waited patiently for the subtext to unfold, but all Mohammed did, with growing intensity, was jump rapidly from one subject to another. His aimless monologue was seemingly intended to delay my departure, for reasons I could not understand. I thought it prudent to get out as fast as I could. When I stood up to thank my host and prepared to leave, Mohammed invited me to stay the night. It was almost midnight, he said smoothly, and the gates of the hotel were likely to be locked. Wouldn't I take advantage of the beautiful rooms and furniture I had helped design? I accepted the offer, foolishly perhaps, and mostly out of curiosity.

As I was settling in for the night I heard the motor of Zubati's car revving, noisily announcing his departure. Soon I heard a light knock on my door. Standing there, dressed in a light nightgown, was Mohammed's wife, looking fearful and harassed. Her voice trembled while she told me that Mohammed had ordered her to impress on me the need to obtain the five hundred pounds promised to him by Abdullah. She apologized for approaching me in that manner and added, "You see what has happened? At first there was no limit to the money he was ready to spend in order to buy my

affection, and now he is ready to sell me to satisfy his greed."
Excusing myself awkwardly, I left the house, wishing I could
have found words to ease the woman's agony. Under these
unusual circumstances it seemed wisest to refrain from further conversation.

Back at the hotel, I thought of Joseph and his encounter with Potiphar's wife:

> One such day, Joseph came into the house to do his
> work, none of the household being there.
> She caught hold of him by his coat and said, "Lie
> with me!" But he left his coat in her hand and got away
> and fled outside.

I silently thanked Mrs. Zubati for her honor and sincerity.

I heard a few weeks later that the women had made another attempt to escape, this time seeking refuge in a house
belonging to Abdullah's cousin, and that Zubati had managed to lure them back home by promising to change his
ways.

And so he did, slowly and gradually. He had begun to
realize that his educated wife was an asset to his growing political career, and therefore to treat her with greater respect.
Under her influence he mastered not only reading and writing but also the art of diplomacy, patience, and greater
respect for others. I sensed an easing of tensions in our relationship too. Mohammed seemed less defensive, less driven,
possibly because he felt less threatened by my friendship
with the emir. He began to pay frequent visits to my house
in Jerusalem, offering gifts of smuggled goods to my wife
and daughter. A transformation was taking place in Mo-

hammed. Much of the change was due to the Syrian teacher who quietly and tactfully succeeded in the education of her husband.

In time, I came to understand Mohammed Zubati better, and I discovered that he was not so very different from many other men I met in the course of my stay in Amman — men equally skillful in their machinations, equally driven by greed for money and power — who treated women in similar fashion. Zubati was simply more direct and possibly more naive. As he learned the ways of the world, however, he began to look and act more like the other, more polished, courtiers. The change may have been no more than skin deep, but it was significant enough to make a difference in the lives of the Syrian bride and her mother, as well as others who came into close contact with the king's right-hand man.

13

Court Intrigue

VILLAINS SCHEMING TO GAIN POWER and grandeur are not in the realm of legends alone. They thrive wherever the rise and fall of a man depends on how well he curries favor with a ruler. And so it was at the court of Abdullah, where people's fortunes rose and fell depending on their ability to scheme.

A man named Subkhi was one such scoundrel. Having just returned from the United States with an engineering degree and enough ambition to make up for his lack of practical experience, Subkhi was appointed assistant to the head of the Department of Public Works. His true goal, however, was to become the emir's personal builder, a position being held by a *yahud*. Subkhi determined first to undermine my position and then to take it.

Subkhi found powerful allies in the officials of the British administration, who were constantly dismayed by Abdullah's excessive expenditures and his penchant for home improvement. They were thus more than happy to have a Jordanian serve as a watchdog over the royal building plans, and issued a regulation requiring that all public construction budgets be approved by Subkhi and his "committee," which essentially consisted of Subkhi alone. He went about carrying out his new responsibility with gusto.

My first run-in with Subkhi involved the building of an apartment for Abdullah's daughter Haya, his firstborn child.

Although both her parents came from noble stock, Haya was not married. She was over thirty — well past marrying age — with no prospect on the horizon. Since she was a member of the nobility, whoever she married had to be of equal status, and available men in this category were few and far between. When she was born, Haya had been promised to Abdullah's nephew Ghazi, crown prince of the Hashemite dynasty in Iraq. Although it was customary for paternal cousins to be promised to each other at birth and to wed when they attained marrying age, Ghazi had defied family tradition and refused to marry Haya. The prince, a flamboyant and independent man, used to make the rounds in Europe, where he had met many women of striking beauty. Haya was relatively unattractive in Ghazi's eyes, and he deemed her unfit for his glamorous lifestyle. In the end Ghazi married another cousin, and was killed in an automobile accident soon afterward.

A second attempt was made to match Haya with a paternal cousin, this time the regent of Iraq and the son of Abdullah's older brother, Ali. That attempt also met with failure. Abdullah, frustrated in finding his daughter a suitor, began to realize that the men of the younger generation were looking for a different breed of women — attractive, well read, and outgoing. While Haya had a pretty face, she was heavy and somewhat clumsy. She was also shy and reserved, and conducted herself with the utmost dignity and self-control. Compared with her jolly half sisters, the daughters of the Minor Emira, Haya seemed somber and distant.

Abdullah was at a loss, because he could not choose a man of lower status. A male member of the nobility might have the option of marrying a woman of lower social standing, because the woman, as Abdullah put it, was "at the bottom of the world" and would play a relatively secondary role in a man's life. The man of the family, however, was the cornerstone of the Islamic world and must keep his honor. Giving his daughter to a man of lesser status would be like bowing to an inferior.

In the absence of appropriate suitors, Abdullah gave up his efforts. Eventually, however, a suitable groom was found. He was a distant cousin, also a Hashemite, who lived in Paris and had not done well financially. He married Haya and was rewarded with a governmental position — that of *Raees el-Diwan*, head of the emir's private office.

I entered the scene when decisions concerning the residence for Haya and her husband were being made. Abdullah was low on funds, as was often the case, but the British agreed to foot the bill up to the sum of fifteen hundred pounds. I was invited to join the directors of the treasury and the Department of Public Works in devising a plan. It was decided to use the allocation to renovate the lower level of the Great Emira's harem, and to turn it into a separate apartment.

The director of the treasury, who had grown up in Damascus, a city known for its tradition of tough bargaining, was hard to deal with. He was ferocious in his attempts to get me to lower my price. Having failed, he turned me over to Mr. Subkhi, who presented me with a contract. This contract was the first ever offered to me while I was in Amman, and it was a true can of worms. The stipulated conditions were wholly impossible to carry out, and I knew immediately that they were designed primarily to prevent successful completion of the work. I could have either refused to accept it and forfeited the job, or accepted it and waited for events to unfold. I chose to go with the latter and signed the contract.

We began the renovation, creating a small but charming apartment for Haya and her husband. The furniture was built in my factory in Jerusalem. When the project was approaching completion, Subkhi appeared on the scene and presented us with a list of changes and modifications that were impossible to implement at that stage. Subkhi made it clear, however, that no payment would be made until all his new specifications were met. My two younger brothers suggested that we forfeit the money and abandon the project, but I insisted that we proceed as planned in spite of Subkhi's objections.

When Abdullah came to see the renovated apartment, he was very satisfied. He took my arm and we walked through the place examining it carefully. As we reached the kitchen we saw Haya hanging curtains that she had embroidered. She smiled and welcomed us to her new home. "It's been a long time since I have seen my daughter smile," Abdullah whispered to me.

I explained some of the technical aspects of the job to Abdullah and used the opportunity to hint at the interference of Subkhi. A master at taking hints, Abdullah picked up the telephone and ordered the director of the treasury to pay me in full. The man on the other end of the line must have mentioned Subkhi and the contract, because Abdullah shouted furiously into the phone, "I don't care about Subkhi and about the contract! Pay him and that's all!"

In the morning I went to see the director. He didn't invite me to sit down nor offer the customary cup of coffee. He wrote a brief note to Prime Minister Tawfiq Abul Huda and asked me to read it. The note said that Sayidna had ordered the *yahud* to be paid regardless of objections on the part of the Department of Public Works and suggested that the prime minister use his own judgment in the matter.

That day I did not have to go through the usual torture of delays when collecting money from the government. To my surprise the prime minister greeted me in a friendly manner, opened his drawer, and gave me a signed check, having obviously been prepared for my arrival by someone other than the director of the treasury or the Department of Public Works. "You are getting it despite the contract," Tawfiq said to me. "What's your secret?"

"I try to do the best job I can at the best price I can for the best man I know," I answered.

When Subkhi heard how the issue had been resolved, he changed his tune. He was building a new house for his family and ordered the furniture through my factory in Jerusalem. I did the best job I could at the best possible price for the person who was not necessarily the best man I knew.

On my daily walks between my temporary residence at the Philadelphia Hotel and Raghdan Palace, I used to stroll along the bank of the stream that flows through the center of Amman. Between the stream and the Roman theater stood a small café, a gathering place for men to pass some time. It was little more than an awning stretched between poles and strung with electric bulbs, which at night shed light on the small tables and stools. At any time, day or night, men could be seen patronizing the café, playing backgammon, leisurely sipping a cold drink, and listening to the trills of a mandolin on the radio. I used to frequent the place initially because of its unusual food and drink. In summer there was *tamar-hindi* (a drink extracted from sweet dates), lemonade, carbonated sour milk, and mint-flavored cold tea. In winter a hot orchid-flavored porridge would be served with fresh *ka-eck*, a donut-shaped bread covered with sesame seeds and garnished with *zaatar*, a ground herb similar to thyme.

My greatest attraction to the place came when I discovered that the court drivers spent much of their free time there. I enjoyed their company because they seemed like a friendly bunch and always had interesting stories to tell. The drivers were mostly urbanized Bedouin who had transferred their love for the camel to its mechanized substitute, the automobile. When I first came to Amman there were few cars on the streets; most transportation was done by horse, camel, or large-wheeled ox carts originally introduced by the Circassians. Within a matter of several years, however, the car became the object of desire not only of the nobility but of the common man. Bedouin who settled in cities and towns poured their hearts and souls into caring for the cars. More than a means of transportation, more than a symbol of riches and status, the four-wheeled vehicle had become to the nomad what his four-legged creature had once been to him — his life.

I found this special breed of people intriguing because

of their gregariousness. All I had to say was *"Shu fi akhbar?"* (what's new?) and the tales began to pour out. They gossiped about everything — except of course the royal harem. A special group of chauffeurs served the women, driving them on shopping trips or bringing female guests to the harem and then returning them to their homes. The drivers were able to look and listen but immediately had to forget anything they had seen or heard. They were categorically forbidden to speak about the women or even to mention their names.

I came to know the drivers well, not only through our contacts at the café but also because they periodically helped out with transportation for me and my crew. In time, I discovered that the rules of discretion about the women depended upon the strictness of the woman's piety and her status in the Hashemite hierarchy. It appeared that the talkativeness of the harem chauffeurs corresponded to the size and thickness of the woman's veil: the thicker the veil, the more circumspect the driver. Thus the chauffeurs of the Great Emira were utterly mute, those serving the Minor Emira permitted themselves a few words or hinted at some incidental detail, and the drivers of Nahada, the emir's third wife, felt free to engage in some gossip.

The drivers had no difficulty telling stories about their own personal lives. They spoke about the tribes and villages from which they came, about places they visited and people they met. They became a major source of information and added significantly to my understanding of Amman and its people.

A driver of great stature at the court was Suliman.

When I first met him, he had served as Abdullah's personal chauffeur for more than ten years. Suliman had all the necessary qualifications for the job — love and respect for the emir and total familiarity with the anatomy of the car. He was a patient and reliable man, always ready for Abdullah's exhausting and unpredictable trips. On a journey away from home he would watch over the car, and often sleep outside wrapped in a blanket.

My friendship with Suliman began fortuitously. He had become engaged to marry a twelve-year-old girl from Ma'an, a town located in southern Transjordan. His meager income enabled him to offer the expected dowry, which he paid in small installments over a two-year period. When the girl turned fourteen, her parents brought her to Amman to marry Suliman, but when they saw his bare apartment, they demanded that he buy a wardrobe for the bride's clothes. They entered into an argument with Suliman about the nature of the wardrobe, bringing the wedding plans to the brink of collapse.

As Suliman was driving me from the palace to my room at the hotel, he told me of his troubles. I offered to help, suggesting that the wardrobe be built for him at my factory in Jerusalem. He was delighted. Not only was he pleased with the design but he found the cost I quoted him surprisingly low. A dark walnut wardrobe decorated with wooden ornaments was built. The bride's family was pleased. The fact that the piece was built by the same *yahud* who was designing the furniture of the emir himself added to their pride, and the issue was thus resolved. The couple were married in a small ceremony attended by friends and relatives. After the ceremony Suliman pulled me aside and said: "You did me a favor I will never forget. I will be indebted to you for the rest of my life."

Suliman managed to save enough money to purchase a piece of land near the stream that runs through Amman. He and his young wife cleared the stones, prepared the soil, seeded, and planted. During his travels with Abdullah, Suliman took the opportunity to collect a variety of exotic plants and turned his property into a little oasis. Selling his plump vegetables at a profit soon enabled Suliman to build a small house on his property.

As Suliman's economic condition improved, his luck took a turn for the worse. Others around the court, and particularly Mohammed Zubati, were beginning to covet his beautiful piece of land. Zubati kept pursuing Suliman to sell him the land, but to no avail. In frustration, Zubati began to taunt Suliman and to accuse him of stealing gasoline from the emir's car. Suliman responded by throwing the car keys in Zubati's face and then punching the monarch's most-favored man. He lost his job as Abdullah's personal chauffeur and never set foot in the court again.

Like a beast stalking its prey, Zubati did not relent. He persuaded the municipality of Amman to build a road that would pass straight through Suliman's property, splitting it in half. Suliman begged Abdullah to intervene and stop the plan, but his plea fell on deaf ears. The emir had no sympathy for those he believed had betrayed him.

When municipal workers came to prepare the ground for the new road, Suliman and his wife stood in their way. Suliman was arrested and thrown into jail. A few months later he was released, looking old and beaten down.

Suliman's resourcefulness and energy, however, returned quickly. He obtained a commission to transfer mail between Jerusalem and Amman. His fortunes rose during the Second World War, when he used his car to transport passengers along with the mail. His company grew, so he hired additional drivers, eventually turning his route into a regular shuttle between the two capitals. The cars were clean, the service was friendly, and the customers kept coming.

I made many friends in Amman, but Suliman had a special place among them. Our friendship grew during the drives between Amman and Jerusalem. We also went on excursions whenever we could find a free day, and he introduced me to different parts of the country. One day, when his car appeared at my house in Jerusalem to take me back to Amman, I saw it was decorated with paper flowers. Suliman emerged, a big grin on his face. "Call me Abu Salim," he announced proudly. He was father of Salim, his firstborn son. "It's all due to you, Khawaja Cohen. I wish I knew how to thank you."

"Don't worry," I replied. "You've done enough." I did not yet foresee the time when Suliman would return the favor manyfold.

14

A King's Lament

WHENEVER ABDULLAH SPOKE OF MECCA AND THE HEJAZ, I could hear a note of longing in his voice, a slight hoarseness. Words would fail him. Here he was, the privileged son of the guardian of the holiest Muslim shrines, ruling over a small Godforsaken land carved out of the desert and inhabited by marauding Bedouin tribes perpetually at war with one another. Neither native to the land nor a member of the local tribes, he had forged a nation out of a collection of nomad clans who roamed the desert in search of grazing. He served them with great devotion and led them wisely, and they, in turn, gradually came to accept his authority.

Only those who knew him well could detect the sadness in his morning prayer. Before dawn, when the palace was in deep slumber, Abdullah would visit his small mosque and chant prayers from the Koran until the sun appeared on the horizon. His voice would fill the air with a deep, sorrowful lament, a call for Allah's compassion, *"Bismillah il Rahman il Rahim"* (In the name of Allah, the Compassionate, the Merciful).

As I came to know him more intimately, I began to

learn more about what lay behind his sadness. He was a man with great aspirations, son of the grand sharif of Mecca. How could he find peace and fulfillment under the thumb of the British Foreign Office in this barren corner of the world?

I began to piece together the pattern of his life the way I put together the pieces of the parquet floor, and came to understand that the self-assured man famous for the twinkle in his eye was not as jubilant as he appeared. He was driven by fierce passions and haunted by deep regrets.

Abdullah was born in 1882 in Mecca. Nestled in a valley surrounded by the rugged hills of western Arabia, Mecca is home to the holy Kaaba, a cube-shaped structure said to have been constructed by Adam and rebuilt by Abraham. Within it is the Black Stone, which, according to the Koran, was a meteorite that came down from heaven and was given to Mohammad by the angel Gabriel so that he could destroy the idols of the infidels. Far from any population centers, Mecca lies close to the heart of every devout Muslim — and to it he turns in prayer five times a day.

It is also the site for a pilgrimage — the hajj — that every true believer must perform once in his life. And because of those pilgrimages Abdullah's eyes were opened to the world, for Mecca was the converging point for multitudes of ethnically diverse pilgrims, each with his own customs and language. From Africa, Java, India, China, the Caucasus, and the Philippines, Muslims come to worship at the holy shrine. Before public transportation was available, great legions of men would gather in Cairo or Damascus during the last month of the Islamic calendar and begin the trek to Mecca by camel. They would bring along goods to trade for food and shelter along the way. Hence religious fervor intermingled with the tumult of commerce and made the hajj the greatest event of a man's life.

When Abdullah spoke about the city and its shrines, his gaze would turn inward. I sensed his love for the *haram* (sacred place) of God. He felt for Mecca what I felt for Jerusalem. For him, it was "where man kills no game, sheds no blood, and uses no unseemly language. Trees may not be pruned within its limits, and fugitives may find refuge there without fear." When a man enters the city he removes his garments, shedding all reminders of rank and ostentation. He dons an *ihram*, a seamless white wrap that makes all men equal before God.

His father, the sharif of Mecca, had been a leader of great honor and responsibility. He kept the city supplied with water and food for the pilgrims, conducted religious services, and distributed commercial licenses. He saw to the safe passage of the pilgrims through the desert route by distributing handsome subventions of gold and goods to the Bedouin sheikhs who determined which pilgrim caravan would be plundered and which would pass safely. As Abdullah once said, "Eighteen hundred purses had to be paid to the Arab tribes who dwelt near the road to ensure safe passage."

Hussein ibn Ali had been an ambitious man. Not only did he fulfill his responsibilities as sharif of the holy shrines and chieftain of the Hejaz with great zeal, but he dreamed of freeing the Hejaz from the yoke of 450 years of Ottoman rule and uniting the whole Arab world under the Hashemite crown.

In 1893 the Turkish sultan Abdul Hamid, suspecting

Hussein of rebellious inclinations, decided to remove him from his base of operations by "inviting" him and his family to live in Constantinople, known today as Istanbul. The sultan made every possible effort to give the sharif and his family a life of comfort and luxury, hoping that Hussein would assimilate into the Turkish culture and renounce his aspirations.

Hussein, his children, his wife, and a party of thirty-two women, along with their suites, settled among other dignitaries on the shores of the Bosphorus, where they lived for fifteen years. When he was old enough, Abdullah became representative of the Hejaz in the Turkish parliament and began to learn his first lessons in Ottoman diplomacy. The early days of the twentieth century were a period of great diversity for cosmopolitan Constantinople, a crossroads between East and West. For Abdullah it provided a window to a world more open and far richer in opportunities than the isolated Hejaz. As he put it, "It was a city of endless fascination, as it gathered many different people — Turks and Arabs, Kurds and Circassians, Egyptians and Sudanese. All fashions and all languages could be found right there. Nothing seemed strange."

In 1908, after fifteen years of exile, Sharif Hussein was granted permission by the sultan to return home to the Hejaz. Initially the sultan had some reservations about letting Hussein go; he was aware of a new courtship developing between the Hashemites and officials of the British Foreign Office in Cairo. Abdullah succeeded, however, in persuading the sultan of his father's loyalty. With an apology for subjecting him to fifteen years of exile, the sultan bestowed on Hussein the title of emir (prince) and grand sharif of

Mecca. As it turned out, the sultan had grossly misjudged the situation.

Sharif Hussein returned to the Hejaz with great pomp and circumstance, an event recounted by Abdullah as one of the most glorious moments in his family's history. Hundreds of notables and important sheikhs came to greet Hussein, whom they addressed as "king of Mecca and sultan of all the Arabs." A procession of Sudanese riflemen, fine horses and camels, and scores of people carrying torches kindled with scented wood followed Hussein to Mecca, singing and chanting. The reception ceremonies lasted for three days and three nights.

Back in the Hejaz, Hussein wasted little time basking in his glory and began working toward his objective: freeing the Hejaz from the Ottoman yoke and unifying the Arab world under Hashemite hegemony. Abdullah, the son best versed in diplomacy and possibly the most intelligent of the four brothers, became the political mastermind behind the process.

Conscious of the rising power of the British and the deterioration of the Ottoman Empire, Abdullah began to look westward. One spring day in 1914, Abdullah called on Lord Kitchener, then British high commissioner in Cairo. Still a member of the Turkish parliament, he did not wish to set an official appointment with a representative of the British government, but he deemed it equally inappropriate to call upon Lord Kitchener unannounced. He decided to ride by Kitchener's home and drop off his card. As luck would have it, the two gentlemen met at the entrance of Kitchener's home and began a "friendly conversation."

More meetings and an exchange of letters ensued. The

essence of the exchange, known as the McMahon Notes, came to constitute the basis for the Hashemite-British alliance. It was agreed that Sharif Hussein would rise in revolt against the Ottoman Empire, and that in return the British would help the Hashemites gain independence in the Hejaz and sovereignty over the Fertile Crescent, referred to as Greater Syria. Unfortunately, and perhaps not accidentally, language concerning the specific boundaries of the territory promised was imprecise, an ambiguity that left much room for different interpretations and became a source of contention between the Arabs and the British for many years to come.

In the middle of the First World War, Hussein and his sons led the people of the Hejaz in a revolt against Turkey. This was called the Arab Revolt of 1916, the starting point of Arab nationalism in the Middle East. Abdullah and his older brother Ali attacked Turkish strongholds in the Hejaz, while Faisal, Abdullah's younger brother, joined the legendary T. E. Lawrence in sabotaging the Damascus-Hejaz railway and causing great damage to the main Turkish supply line. Faisal later entered Damascus on the heels of the British army with his camel-riding caravan. When the war ended in 1918, Faisal was crowned king of Syria and Hussein assumed the title "king of the Hejaz." Abdullah remained at his father's side in the position of foreign minister, charged with the responsibility of negotiating the final terms of the British-Hashemite agreement.

Although Abdullah and his father shared the same ambition, the two men differed in fundamental ways and did not get along. Hussein was somber, intense, contentious, and quick to anger; Abdullah was affable, full of verve, optimistic, and a prankster at times. While Hussein often turned to military means to resolve differences, Abdullah believed in the power of the word. In their political wheeling and dealing, Hussein, in true tribal tradition, used oblique signals, devious language, and ambiguities, while Abdullah, exposed to the West, was more pragmatic and thus more flexible.

The tensions between Abdullah and his father came to a head at the end of the war, when it was time to implement earlier agreements with the British government. It appeared that the British were reneging on their promises with regard to a Hashemite-ruled Greater Syria. It was soon discovered that the British and the French had already reached a secret agreement about the former Ottoman Empire, dividing the spoils of war between them, leaving only portions of the territory to the Hashemites.

Abdullah, the realist, attempted to negotiate a compromise, but Hussein would accept nothing short of the total package, namely, full sovereignty over the Fertile Crescent. In his anger and frustration, Hussein blamed his son for failing to take a tough stand with the British, for being politically naive, and for having become a Westernized softy, lacking the *shatara* (nerve) of a true Bedouin. Abdullah, on the other hand, attributed the stalemated negotiations to his father's rigid grandiosity, which left him no room to maneuver.

Abdullah never regained his father's full respect and approval, even when he had become sovereign of his own state. When Abdullah was named emir of Transjordan, his father expressed little confidence in his capacity to lead.

I heard a story recounted at the court about an incident

that took place shortly after the establishment of Abdullah's government in Amman. Hussein had come to visit and, apparently, overstayed his welcome. He made policy, met with dignitaries, and attempted to tutor his son in the business of running a country, while Abdullah, out of respect for his father, did little to resist his interference. It was evident to his British patrons that Abdullah's authority was being undermined at its inception. When they realized that the old patriarch, generally sensitive to the slightest nuance, was failing to register rather obvious hints, they determined to nudge him out of Transjordan. A young British officer by the name of Alec Kirkbride, who was to become British ambassador to Jordan, was assigned the task. Kirkbride, deeply distressed at the prospect of facing Hussein's unbridled rage, made inquiries — and learned that the train that had brought Hussein to Transjordan had been undergoing repairs, but now was again ready for operation. He simply informed Hussein that the train would be ready to take him back home the next day. This time Hussein got the message. He boarded the train twenty-four hours later.

In spite of the scorn and humiliation Abdullah experienced at the hands of his father, he shared his father's dream and was deeply committed to its legacy. In fact he was driven by the conviction that the Hashemites, descendants of the Prophet, were destined to gather the peoples of the Arab world under their crown. Yet he lived with the somber awareness that he had failed to achieve this glorious dream. A part of him never gave up his father's grand ambition, and a part knew that he had to accept compromises. Caught between these two poles, he remained forever deprived of his father's accolades.

I felt great respect for Abdullah's energy and his vast reservoir of optimism, and grew to appreciate them more fully as I came to recognize the sadness behind them.

I remember that there was a sword leaning against the back wall of the royal tent, larger than the other swords and engraved with an inscription. It had been a subject of my curiosity for some time, but I was unable to get close enough to examine it without appearing rude. Though I caught a quick glimpse of it every time I entered the tent, there was never time to read the inscription. The emir once caught me looking at the sword.

"Nice sword?" he asked with a smile.

"Yes, *ya sayidi*. I have admired its beauty for some time and observed it has something written on it."

"It was given to me by my father after the war with the Wahabi tribe," he replied.

"In honor of your triumph!" I exclaimed.

"No, no. We lost that battle, but my father gave it to me anyway," he said, quickly calling my attention to a set of blueprints we were planning to examine together.

Abdullah was not a man inclined to dwell upon defeats, nor to expose personal failures and vulnerabilities. I raised the subject of the Wahabis very gingerly, and learned only bits and pieces about his military defeat and the loss of the Hejaz. Most of what I learned came from those in Amman willing to defy the unspoken taboo against discussing the private life of the monarch and his family.

Before the dawning of the twentieth century, most of the Arabian Peninsula consisted of barren hills and desert valleys where tribes of nomad Bedouin roamed in search of grazing for their herds of goats and camels. The Hashemites and the Saudis were among the more prosperous of the tribes that had given up nomadic existence and settled in roughly delineated areas of the peninsula, establishing towns, cities, and permanent encampments. The Saudis dominated central Arabia, a land called Nejd, and the Hashemites western Arabia, the Hejaz. The two major clans lived in their respective areas, alternately in harmony and conflict with each other, until a struggle for the domination of greater Arabia and the holy shrines of Mecca and Medina began to escalate.

Isolated deep in the Arabian desert, the Saudi clan retained a fundamentalist view of the Koran and a strict approach to its interpretation. The Hashemites, who lived near the sea and on the routes of pilgrimages to the holy center of Islam, came into repeated contact with peoples of different backgrounds and thus were more tolerant of diversity and more flexible in their religious orientation. They viewed the Saudis as primitive zealots, uninformed and closed-minded, while the Saudis saw their Hejazi neighbors as irreverent and negligent in their adherence to the tenets of the Koran.

Between Nejd and the Hejaz lived a group of nomads called Wahabis, whose reading of the Koran was even more literal than that of the Saudis. Under the protection of the Saudis, they organized into communities that served as bases for their religious wars and a launching point for Saudi expansionism. The Wahabis were fired by the belief that they alone were true Muslims and that it was their sacred duty to return to Allah all those who had strayed, even if it meant putting every male to the sword. Their passion and reckless courage made them fierce warriors, ready to sacrifice their lives for the place in paradise reserved for those who fought in a holy war. For years they plundered villages and tribes across the Arabian Peninsula, Iraq, and Transjordan, killing many.

Combined with Wahabi religious zeal, Saudi territorial aspirations represented a threat too great for the Hashemites to ignore. Following a series of unsuccessful campaigns to keep the Wahabis in check, Sharif Hussein decided to wage an all-out war to wipe them out and to defeat their Saudi protectors. Abdullah was named chief commander of the expedition.

Abdullah tried to dissuade his father from pursuing war. "The Wahabis are fanatic warriors, and much blood will flow," he argued. Hussein, however, kept insisting that an army be raised for the operation. "Is this an opinion or a command?" Abdullah asked, exasperated. It was a command.

In May 1919 Abdullah organized an army of two thousand warriors and moved his camp close to Wahabi territory. The Wahabis gathered a camel-riding force of several thousand. Before dawn, while Abdullah's army was asleep, the banner- and bayonet-waving Wahabis spurred their camels toward Abdullah's camp, took it by surprise, and killed most of the men. While his slaves were fighting to protect his tent from the front, Abdullah cut a hole in the rear and fled on his horse, with barely his shirt on. As he was galloping away, he heard the cries of the Wahabis, mocking him for his small stature, "The short one! The short one!"

Following the destruction of the Hashemite army, the Saudis continued to press on. In 1924 Hussein abdicated his crown and went into exile in Cyprus, never to return to his homeland. Within a year the Saudis had conquered all of the Hejaz and taken over control of the Muslim holy places. Mecca and Medina and the future oil riches of Arabia were lost to the Hashemites forever.

Whenever Abdullah mentioned the Saudis I could see smoldering rage in his eyes and the furrows of pain on his forehead. I knew that he had signed a treaty with the Saudis only a few years earlier, but I also knew that the peace agreement had not brought inner peace.

One night he spoke the name of Ibn Saud in anger.

"Ya sayidi," I asked him, "didn't you sign a treaty with Ibn Saud? Didn't you settle your differences? And after all, doesn't the Arabic saying go, 'One day for you and one day against you'?"

He stood up at the opening of his tent and, looking far into the Syrian Desert, shouted, *"Abadan!* — never! They robbed us of our right to the holy cities given to us by our Prophet!"

I felt a chill go down my spine. Would he utter the same words again when the time came to determine the future of Jerusalem?

15

Life Under the Inglizi

THE AFTERMATH OF THE ARAB REVOLT and the victory
over the Ottomans did not bring about the realization
of the Hashemite dream. Hussein's army had been badly defeated by the Wahabis and the British were in no hurry to
rebuild it. Relations between Abdullah and his father were
deteriorating, and the British were getting tired of old Hussein's intransigence and grand schemes. It was also becoming evident to Abdullah that his younger brother Faisal was
replacing him as spokesman of the Hashemites in the international arena. Abdullah needed a new base of operations
for his political future.

Abdullah had two major objectives in mind when he
left his father. First was his desire to find his own place in
the world. Second, perhaps no less important, was his desire
to right the wrong endured by his brother Faisal at the
hands of the French. When the victorious allies were
parceling out the Middle East at the end of the First World
War, the British placed Faisal at the helm of Syria, but the
French, who took over Syria a little later, had no intention
of retaining a British-sponsored monarch on their territory.

When they entered Damascus they expelled Faisal after a brief military confrontation.

In 1920 Abdullah left the Hejaz with several hundred soldiers and headed north on the Damascus-Hejaz railway. The railway was a legend in its own time. Construction on it had begun in 1900, to celebrate the twenty-fifth anniversary of Sultan Abdul Hamid's reign. It had required enormous financial resources and taken eight years to complete. Turkey, Egypt, and Iraq each contributed $250,000, and every resident of the Ottoman Empire was taxed 10 percent of one month's salary and five gold coins. Built according to the latest technology, the railway transported thousands of pilgrims between Damascus and Medina every year.

But when Abdullah boarded the train in 1920, most of the luxury features were long gone. The rails had been severely damaged during the war by the forces of T. E. Lawrence and Sharif Hussein's sons, assisted by Bedouin who willingly joined in the destruction of the railway that had rendered the pilgrim-carrying camel obsolete. Abdullah and his small army had to stop frequently along the way to repair the rails and collect discarded telegraph poles, remnants of trees, and shrubs to feed the train's fuel box. It took twenty-seven days to cross a distance that normally took no more than two, but the arduous trip did little to diminish Abdullah's determination. He made his first official stop in Ma'an, a town in southern Transjordan, which was part of the Hejaz at the time.

Transjordan was then a sparsely populated area of endless deserts and arid mountains, situated east of the Jordan River, north of the Red Sea port of Aqaba, and south of the

Yarmuk River. When Abdullah arrived, it was populated by no more than 250,000 people. More than half the population consisted of Bedouin tribes who roamed the desert and were at perpetual war with one another, looting and plundering as a major means of subsistence. The Bedouin called no place home, and paid no mind to international boundaries or nationalities, reserving their loyalty only to their families, clans, tribal chiefs, and their prophet Mohammed.

There was a small group of fellahin, or peasants, who populated the more fertile parts of the Jordan Valley and the north. They lived under the constant threat of the Bedouin, who used to plunder and loot their villages. In the absence of even the ineffective protection the Ottoman police had provided, they were forced to pay handsome sums to the Bedouin grandees for protection. The Bedouin considered themselves aristocrats of the desert, the true Arabs, and looked with disdain on the fellahin. The fellahin considered the Bedouin no more than marauders who needed to be kept at bay.

A yet smaller group of merchants and peddlers lived in squalid little towns, carving out a meager living from petty commerce characterized by corruption and inefficiency, true to the legacy of Ottoman rule.

When Abdullah reached his first stop in Transjordan, the tribesmen in the area gathered around the station to greet him and kiss the hem of his robe. Abdullah called on them to unite, eloquently exclaiming, "Cease to think of yourselves as separate tribes, that you may learn to be loyal to the Great Arab Brotherhood that embraces us all." He urged them to join together to liberate Syria. "I am proud to join in your defense and drive the French aggressors from your shores.

We call upon you to unite and resist anyone who might weaken your resolve." The Bedouin rallied around the son of the grand sharif of Mecca, descendant of the Prophet.

Having established his first successful contact with the local population in the south, Abdullah moved northward to Kerak, in a no-man's land called Moab governed by the British. Alec Kirkbride, then governor of the territory, rode out to meet Abdullah and welcome him, but as he had been given no instructions from Whitehall, he had no idea how to deal with the man.

"Did you come to welcome me on behalf of His Majesty's Government of Great Britain?" asked Abdullah.

"Well, hmm . . ." Kirkbride replied hesitantly. "I am here to welcome the emir on behalf of the Government of Moab."

That was good enough for Abdullah, who took Kirkbride's words to imply official British recognition of his suzerainty in Transjordan. That meeting was the beginning of a thirty-year friendship between Abdullah and Kirkbride, and the first step toward a Hashemite foothold in the area.

Abdullah moved farther north to establish a government. The attack on Syria never took place. The Bedouin fighting spirit petered out when Abdullah's empty coffers could no longer nurture their combativeness. Furthermore, the British were putting pressure on him to restrain the Bedouin near the Syrian border, because they did not wish to enter into territorial disputes with their French allies. Abdullah had to abandon his efforts to liberate Syria. He concentrated on setting up a provisional government in Amman.

In 1921 a meeting took place in Jerusalem between

Abdullah and Winston Churchill, then Britain's colonial secretary, to finalize the British-Hashemite agreement. Churchill opened the meeting by extolling the noble aims that had united the British and the Arabs during the war, then proceeded to lay out the essence of his government's plan: Faisal, who had recently lost the throne of Syria, would be offered the monarchy of Iraq and would have to be crowned immediately to forestall a Saudi claim to the same throne; Hussein would remain king of the Hejaz; and Abdullah would be proclaimed emir of Transjordan, an area previously considered part of Palestine.

Abdullah's attempts to negotiate for the incorporation of the land west of the river into his domain were thwarted, as the area had already been promised to the Jews as a national home. Churchill's offer was a far cry from what Abdullah aspired to, but his protestations did little to move the colonial secretary. Churchill had his mind made up. He closed the meeting by saying, "I am afraid I have tired you. I shall look forward to your reply tomorrow morning." Abdullah could take it or leave it.

The pragmatic Abdullah accepted Churchill's proposal. As the Hashemite brothers often reminded each other, the wisest course was to take everything they could and wait for tomorrow, "because nights are pregnant and might give birth to miracles." But a miracle was not born during the night. Abdullah was declared the official emir of the new semi-independent state of Transjordan, under the supervision of a British mandate.

From an Arab perspective, Churchill's resolution was a violation of their rights, a betrayal of the agreements reached with the British during the war. To the Hashemite family it meant a dissolution of their dream of ruling over a unified nation, embracing Iraq, Syria, Lebanon, Palestine, and Transjordan. During one of his frank moments Abdullah expressed his feelings over the British betrayal to me. "I joined my father during the Arab Awakening to create a united Arab Kingdom. And look at what happened. We were balkanized and even the little countries they carved for us are not independent. So what was the point of replacing one master with another?" I had often heard Arabs in both Transjordan and Israel express a similar belief — that the Arabs would have become a single nation had the British not divided them into smaller countries. But I wondered whether the Arabs, internally divided between fanatics and moderates, Sunni and Shiites, pro- and anti-Western, republicans and monarchists, could ever have become one nation.

The division of the British mandate into Palestine and Transjordan was as painful to us as it was to the Arabs of the region. For Jews, it was a violation of a sacred promise made by the British and the League of Nations. Established in 1919, the mandate incorporated the objectives and language of the Balfour Declaration, which read as follows:

His Majesty's Government view with favour the establishment in Palestine of a national home for the Jewish people, and will use their best endeavours to facilitate the achievement of this object, it being clearly understood that nothing shall be done which may prejudice the civil and religious rights of existing non-Jewish communities in Palestine or the rights and political status enjoyed by Jews in any other country.

I still remember when the British general Sir Edmund Allenby entered Jerusalem a month later. The Ottomans were losing the war and the Jewish community in Jerusalem was in great jeopardy. People were succumbing to hunger and disease, and those still alive were facing deportation by the Turkish government. The Jews of Jaffa had already been expelled; the Jews living in the Old City were the next target. In marched General Allenby through the Jaffa Gate of Jerusalem at that low moment of dread, with his infantry and bagpipe fifes. At the time the British were seen as liberators.

When Sir Herbert Samuel was appointed the first high commissioner of Palestine, we walked around as if in a dream. "He is a Jew," we said, "a true advocate for our community at the highest echelons of government." It did not take long, however, for disillusionment to set in. In 1922, the British government issued a white paper report announcing that Transjordan would be excluded from the area intended as a Jewish homeland. We didn't know then that the division of Palestine along the Jordan River would be only the first in a series of acts that would curtail Jewish immigration and repeatedly shrink the size of the Jewish state.

Despite my feelings over the partition and despite our different national aspirations, I viewed Abdullah's accomplishments with awe. He had come as a stranger to a country that had minimal natural resources and was home to a tribal society divided by feuds and war. Governmental institutions were either nonexistent or decaying. There was no nation to behold. However, by the time I went to Transjordan only fifteen years later, many of the Bedouin had been "acculturated." Some were still partly nomadic, while others had given up nomadic life altogether and settled into urban communities or farming villages. A few had joined the army and/or police force or held civil service and governmental jobs.

I often heard Abdullah express his impatience with the rate of progress in his country, comparing it unfavorably with the accomplishments of the Jewish community of Palestine. He envied us and resented us at the same time. Did he fail to see that in our own way we were engaged in an endeavor much like his own? As different as we were, Arabs and Jews were walking parallel paths, both involved in forging our own national identity. I wonder now what I wondered then: whether it would ever come to pass that we would learn from each other and live in peace as neighbors.

Shortly after I first came to Amman, Abdullah showed me a letter he had received from Sir Henry Cox, the British representative to Jordan, better known as the Resident. The Resident objected to my employment at the court and questioned "the advisability of the practice at a time of great peril." Cox's personal disapproval of the employment of Jews from Palestine was supported by a British law prohibiting "foreigners" from settling in Transjordan. Abdullah had no intention of responding to the letter, let alone heeding its content. He handed the letter to me, saying, "Read what *your Inglizi* are saying." He did not yet know that the Inglizi were no more mine than his.

Cox's resentment over my continued presence at the court turned into open anger. The fact that my building projects entailed further expenditures fueled Cox's rancor. He never acknowledged me and used to look the other way when he chanced to see me. I learned to ignore him too. The Resident's wife, who spoke Arabic fluently and was a frequent visitor to the women's quarters, treated me with the same coldness.

Hence I was surprised one day when Lady Cox asked me to take on the job of packing her more valuable belongings and shipping them home to England. She told me that she had greater confidence in me than in the "local labor." She gave no thought to the fact that Abdullah was standing within earshot, listening to her characterization of Arab workers. My response to her was clear and blunt. I replied that I had no interest in working for people who did not desire my presence. It is not my habit to engage in vendetta, but this time I couldn't resist. As Lady Cox turned away in anger, I saw out of the corner of my eye a subtle smile of satisfaction on Abdullah's face.

It was becoming increasingly evident to me that Abdullah also felt no affection for Sir Henry — that we shared the same feelings about the British government and its representative. Only later, when he felt freer to express his opinion, did Abdullah describe the years of Cox's residency as "difficult times for Transjordan and the Hashemite family. Cox liked to work with those with whom he felt at ease, and much patience was required." This was Abdullah's way of saying that Cox liked to associate only with people of his own kind.

Personal incompatibility between Cox and Abdullah was not at the core of the emir's resentment. The more fundamental bitterness involved issues of sovereignty and control. While he had a number of genuine friends in the British administration, Abdullah felt betrayed by His

Majesty's Government, which had reneged on its political promises and exercised undue control over the affairs of his state.

During the early stages of his suzerainty the British demonstrated little confidence in Abdullah's ability to govern. Their concern stemmed to a great extent from Abdullah's difficulties in managing the budget and staying within the limits of the subsidy provided by Whitehall. Although the British financial allotment increased manyfold in the course of a few years, Abdullah was forever short of funds and constantly requiring supplementary support.

Of course the issue of money, while central and vexing, masked a far bigger issue. The British mandate government reserved ultimate control over all matters, be they international, local, or personal, including some of Abdullah's truly private affairs. My workers and I could not cross the border or transfer building materials for the palace without first obtaining a permit issued by the Resident. Foreign currency needed for the importation of goods was allocated by the Resident's office — usually in the quality of personal favors, and too often used for the purchase of expensive cars and other luxury items, with little regard for the needs of the economy.

So nowhere were the British more invasive than in Abdullah's monetary affairs. Having a fundamentally different view of the use of public money, the British simply could not conceive of Abdullah's fiscal system, which mixed private and governmental funds to build personal homes and palaces, nor understand the need for the large sums of money he distributed among the Bedouin chiefs. Abdullah, on the other hand, saw these traditional expenditures as the most efficient way to maintain the loyalty of his citizens. And while he used public funds to finance personal projects, he was equally generous in using personal funds to finance public services.

During the summer month Abdullah used to sit outside the Diwan under a fig tree, his favorite cat purring at his feet. People used to come to seek his advice or to lodge complaints. One day a weeping sharecropper and his wife came to him for help. The man kissed the hem of the emir's robe and proceeded to tell him of his woes. Because of their advancing age he and his wife were no longer able to hold on to the piece of land leased to them by the effendi and had been deprived of their only means of livelihood. Abdullah listened intently, then dug into his own pockets, only to discover that they were empty. He pulled the rug out from beneath him, rolled it up, and gave it to the old man. For Abdullah, doing this was second nature. As the Koran has it, "the likeness of those who spend their wealth in the way of Allah is as the likeness of a grain that sprouts seven spikes, in every spike a hundred grains." To his British patrons, however, this was a conspicuously bizarre way to run a state.

In 1924 the British attempted to get rid of Abdullah and replace him with a more financially conservative administrator. However, given Abdullah's success in bringing the populace under control and in ending internal warfare, Whitehall decided to retain him and to appoint a Resident to oversee his affairs. A number of Residents came and went, none of whom could succeed in putting Abdullah's affairs in order.

British concern over Abdullah's style of money management may not have been altogether unfounded. I often heard Abdullah complain about his deficit, and yet immediately request that I procure for him some expensive item he could not afford. At times I had to restrain Abdullah's tendency to spend large sums of money, and try to scale down his construction plans; he rarely thought of doing so himself. His need to demonstrate his power through grand gestures often left him in dire financial straits.

I remember one story from Abdullah himself:

"During the Arab Revolt of the Hashemites against Turkey," he began, "the commander of a Turkish garrison near Mecca, Farkhi Pasha, was captured. Farkhi and I had served together in the Turkish army and we had been good friends. When I heard that Farkhi was among the prisoners, I went to see him immediately and found him deeply shaken by rage and humiliation. To lighten the situation I jokingly reminded him that he had once given my brother a pair of field glasses as a gift and totally overlooked me. To my surprise, Farkhi reached into his jacket, pulled out his own field glasses, and handed them to me. I was deeply touched. I took off my wrist watch and gave it to him. It was a precious watch given to me by my brother Ali. It was made of gold with a blue enamel face and pink shading resembling the rays of the sun, and engraved with my brother's name. I saw tears of gratitude in Farkhi's eyes. At first he refused to accept the watch, but he agreed to do so when I said that I was only following our great Arab tradition."

The British were hardly impressed by similar manifestations of this "great Arab tradition," especially when they were the ones underwriting the expense. They instructed

Sir Henry Cox either to curb the man's munificence or get rid of him. Unable to restrain Abdullah, Cox was determined to unseat him. When the emir was out of the country, a small British force was stationed in Amman with orders to block his return. Abdullah's homecoming, however, coincided with the victory of the Arab Legion over a force of invading Saudis, and Amman was filled with jubilant crowds cheering their leader. It was the least opportune time for Cox to carry out his plan. The coup was shelved.

Alec Kirkbride, who had first welcomed Abdullah when he entered Transjordan, took over as Resident when Cox retired. Kirkbride was instrumental in laying to rest the furor over the budget, pointing out to his government that a military-political base consisting of a British command and a local army inspired by a loyal indigenous ruler was far more efficient and less costly than deploying British troops in Transjordan. The British came to accept Abdullah's lack of financial restraint as a necessary evil, and Abdullah continued to live in a permanent state of debt.

Kirkbride's residency was a time of close cooperation with Britain and of great progress for the country. In 1946, when Transjordan was declared the independent Hashemite Kingdom of Jordan and Abdullah its king, Kirkbride became Jordan's first British ambassador. Abdullah and Kirkbride had taken to each other from the moment they first met and came to understand each other very well. Kirkbride was always careful never to hurt Abdullah's pride, while Abdullah was quick to understand Kirkbride's implicit messages. When Kirkbride said, "His Majesty's Government hopes that Your Majesty would accept its advice," Abdullah would understand that there was room for negotiation, but if Kirkbride added, "and I hope you will accept," it meant that the British position had to be accepted without dissent.

At times even words were unnecessary. I once saw Abdullah emerge from a meeting quite perturbed. When I asked him why, he replied that he had just left the meeting because the *tawil* (the tall one, meaning Kirkbride) was about to reject the idea of building a new road connecting Amman and Shuneh.

"Why?" I asked. "What did he say?"

"He didn't say anything, but he moved forward in his seat, as he usually does when he is about to say 'no.' I don't have to wait for him to actually tell me that His Majesty's Government regrets this and that."

I often wondered about the friendship between Kirkbride and Abdullah. As amiable and supportive as he was, Kirkbride was nonetheless a representative of a colonizing foreign body, and given to the patronizing affectations so typical of many of his countrymen. I was never sure of the real feelings held by the tall smiling Inglizi toward his king, nor of Abdullah's private thoughts about his foreign benefactor.

Abdullah's resentment was usually cloaked by his jovial gregariousness. He knew full well that he could not survive without British support. Transjordan would have been overrun by the Saudis had it not been for British intervention. Without the British-led Arab Legion, tribal strife would have splintered the country into bits. The government would have gone broke and Abdullah into bankruptcy were it not for the British exchequer. So he kept his bitterness to himself and continued to extend his friendship and hospitality in true Bedouin fashion.

Resentment, however, would break through once in a while. I remember one incident when Abdullah couldn't contain his anger toward his friend Kirkbride. We were about to launch a large construction project and I was looking for ways to keep costs down. This was during the Second World War, when the British were constructing new roads and bridges, consuming a major portion of building materials in the region. Amman was undergoing a boom, since many of its citizens had accumulated small fortunes through smuggling and other war-related businesses, and they were investing their profits in the construction of new homes and commercial properties. The price of building materials, especially cement, was skyrocketing. I called Abdullah's attention to the fact that cement produced by Nesher, a Jewish company in Haifa, was less than a quarter of its cost in Amman, and proposed that we import the cement for his new project. All we needed, I suggested, was a permit issued by the Resident. I knew I had touched a raw nerve when Abdullah blurted out in anger, "I don't want to ask the *tawil* for any favors. I would rather pay more than demean myself in front of that Englishman."

In their imperial arrogance the British failed to see all the facets of Abdullah's character. Particularly during the early days of his rule, they perceived him as somewhat of a lightweight — exotic, princely, and entertaining, but in essence a "native" from the Arabian hinterland, unprepared to assume the reins of a country that barely existed in the first place. Only those who saw through his convivial manner came close to recognizing his ability to stay the course. I had great respect for his determination and drive, but as an outsider sharing the perspective of the Jewish community in Israel, I often watched them with a sense of unease and wariness.

16

The British Brigadier and the Bedouin King

I T WAS MY FRIEND SULIMAN THE DRIVER — before his dismissal — who suggested that we venture into the desert in his car. He wanted to show me a piece of the past, he told me, the way things used to be before his people gave up their nomadic life and settled in Amman. I gladly accepted. Early one morning, before the sun began its relentless assault on the desert plain, we were off into the Syrian Desert. Stretching over an area that reaches into Syria in the north, Iraq in the east, and Saudi Arabia in the south, the desert steppe rises between two and three thousand feet above sea level. As the car climbed eastward toward the top of the plain, the rising sun hit the windshield, blinding us with its intensity. While I could hardly see in front of me, Suliman was not a bit fazed by the glare; he knew every twist and turn and every creek and valley that crisscrossed the plain.

"I am going to take you by the route used by the Arab Legion when they crossed the desert on their way to Baghdad," announced Suliman.

The Baghdad campaign was a saga recounted with great pride by the people of Transjordan. At the beginning of the Second World War, Abdullah cabled Winston

Churchill and offered him the services of the Arab Legion. The offer was politely declined, owing to the British lack of confidence in an army of Bedouin who had only recently. emerged out of nomadic life, particularly if it was to be led by John Bagot Glubb. The British viewed their compatriot "Glubb Pasha" as a hopeless romantic.

In 1941, a German sympathizer by the name of Rashid Ali toppled the pro-British government of Iraq. Worried about a German takeover and the threat that would pose to the Suez Canal, Churchill asked for the assistance of the Arab Legion in guiding a British contingent through the Syrian Desert to Baghdad.

"They used to call them Glubb's Girls, but they had no idea how tough it was to cross this desert." Suliman was referring to the British ridicule of the Arab Legion warriors, who wore gowns and braided their long hair. "They couldn't have done it without us. They would have died of thirst if we hadn't led them to water. They had no way of knowing the right trails. Or which sheikhs they could trust and who should be avoided. And when the British heavy trucks sank into the sand, who do you think pulled them out? We were the first to enter Baghdad, with the British trailing behind!"

I couldn't tell how much of Suliman's story was factual and how much a product of Bedouin hyperbole. I didn't doubt, however, that in their smug attitude the British had grossly underestimated the valor and discipline of the most effective Arab army in the Middle East. The Arab Legion had kept the borders of Transjordan intact, protected the personal safety of their monarch, and played a major role in transforming a tribal culture into a unified nation. (Little did I know that in a few years this celebrated legion would bombard my home, capture the Old City of Jerusalem, and destroy its synagogues.)

"We will soon reach one of the old citadels used as a shelter by Glubb and his army during their passage. Some of the citadels were actually built by the Romans and later rebuilt by the Umayyad caliphs who came from Baghdad. They used these castles as hunting lodges, but as you will see, there was more to it than hunting. The caliphs used them to escape the strict rules of the Koran, drinking wine and enjoying other carnal pleasures. You will see!"

Approaching Qasr el-Amra, I could sense Suliman's excitement grow. A slight push of the door opened the castle to us, and we walked into the dark cool of the interior. We waited for our eyes to adjust to the darkness. Suliman turned his flashlight on the floor, walls, and ceilings, trying to find spots that were not covered with soot. Little by little I began to realize that the site was a treasure of unimaginable dimensions. The *qasr* had several vaults, each with its own unique mosaic floor, wall murals, and painted ceiling. Some depicted nude women bathing, scenes of love, music making, hunters chasing after boar and gazelle, and the bounty of grapes and wine. As we walked through the vaults, I discovered that one room had been used as a steam bath, another had provided tepid water, and a third fresh cold water, all fed by underground springs that had long since dried up. The ceiling of the steam room depicted a star-studded sky with its constellations. Enough of it was visible through the layers of dirt to tease the imagination and guess at its beauty.

"The Umayyad believed that lovemaking emptied the

body and that the baths helped restore it," Suliman told me as we walked out.

Squinting in the bright sun, we returned to the car for a drink of water, which by now was lukewarm from the heat. This was the first water we had had since we left earlier that morning. Suliman only wet his lips, drinking very little. It was considered a mark of valor for Bedouin to drink as little of the precious water as their beloved camels.

As we drove north toward the Syrian border, the longest stretches of the desert still lay ahead of us, barren and parched. "You know some Bedouin still roam the plains for a little grass and a few drops of water. We've done it for generations. But can you imagine an Englishman riding this whole way on a camel for many days? That's what Abu Hanik did."

Abu Hanik was the name used by the Bedouin when they were referring approvingly to John Glubb. It meant "father of the small chin." His disfigured chin was the result of a wound incurred during the First World War. When he became commander of the Arab Legion, he acquired the honorific title of pasha.

"Did I ever tell you how Glubb Pasha came to be commander of the Legion? It's quite a story. Having succeeded in calming some of the warring tribes in Iraq, he took a camel ride across the desert to Amman. He paid a visit to Abdullah's palace, where he encountered Abdullah's father, who had recently arrived from the Hejaz. When Hussein heard of Glubb's long camel ride from Iraq, he was so impressed that he grabbed Glubb's hand, shook it, and exclaimed, *'Wellahi, hada Bedoui!'* [By God, this one is a Bedouin!] Only a few days earlier Hussein had also taken a desert trip on a camel. They say that Sayidna, trying to make things easier for his aging father, sent a car to fetch him at the border, but that the old man had refused to ride in the car. He preferred to ride his camel to the nearest train station, a hundred miles away. When Abdullah met Glubb he knew that his father had been right. The Englishman was a Bedouin at heart. He was the right man for the job — the job of commanding Abdullah's police force, which became the Arab Legion."

Just as I was beginning to absorb the real meaning of a camel ride in this forbidding climate, Suliman stopped the car in front of a black Bedouin tent. The tent was no more than a black strip of woven goat's wool hung on three poles. An old Bedouin emerged from within and greeted us with a wave of the hand and a wide toothless smile. He invited us to come in and have a cup of coffee. His name was Khaled and he belonged to the Suwaiti clan, one of the fiercest in the past and now one of the poorest. As I looked around, I saw the familiar curtain dividing the tent into men's and women's quarters and could hear the women banging their pots and pans, obviously involved in the preparation of food. The tent was furnished with only few belongings — a colorful rug woven of sheep's wool and a few pots and mattresses piled up in the corner. With measured movements Khaled built a small fire outside the tent and boiled a pot of bitter coffee, which he then served in small brass cups. He asked that we stay for the evening meal. There would not be much, he said, just some lamb and cheese. As I looked at the small herd of sheep outside, I realized that he was offering us a major part of his small fortune. We naturally declined, but Khaled begged us to stay as if his life depended on it. I never found it so hard to decline an invitation as I did that afternoon.

We drove farther into the desert, through fields of small black pebbles. *Hamada*, they call it. The dry afternoon wind blew gray sand into our car. Suliman shut the car windows to shield us from the dust, but the interior of the car was no more comfortable, as it had already absorbed much of the desert heat. We had driven only about a mile or two northward when Suliman stopped the car and stepped out. I followed. "Now I want to show you my country. See this desert? That's where my people came from — Wadi Sirhan. Over there," he said, pointing southward, "were endless wars between the tribes and our people lost many men in battle. Finally my father gave up and joined the Arab Legion. There he learned to read and write and then moved to Amman and became a driver, like me."

"It must have been pretty wild, living like that, always moving and always fighting the next tribe," I commented.

"No, not wild at all. All these wars were fought according to rules. When raiding an enemy encampment the raiders would strike at dawn rather than at night, to make sure they didn't hurt women and children. And at the *sulkha* when peace was reached, casualties were compensated according to a fixed schedule. The price of a tribesman's life was higher than that of a slave, and that of a chief greater than that of a warrior."

Suliman's back straightened with pride. "And the *amyria*? Did you ever hear about that? I have never seen it, but I heard my father tell about it. When the men gathered for war, the tribal maidens would mount the tribe's camels, which were gaily decorated for the event, and then ride into the middle of the warriors. In the heat of battle they would stand up on the camel's back, let their hair down and bare their breasts, flick their tongues on the roof of their mouths to produce sharp trills, and call individual warriors by name to spur them on. And if a maiden happened to be captured by the enemy, it was only honorable to bring her back to her tribe unharmed."

I listened to the young man spinning his stories in rich Arabic, articulating his experiences with skill and enthusiasm. He showed no signs of fatigue and was in full control of the vehicle and the desert around him. As we drove back into Amman, I thought of the transition that had occurred in Transjordan since the arrival of Abdullah.

Suliman was part of the world that had changed. His tribesmen were no longer tent dwellers, no longer nomads moving back and forth across the desert. They had settled on farms and in cities, employed as drivers, cooks, craftsmen, and civil servants. Much of this change, which occurred in just two decades, was due to the combined efforts of the emir and Glubb Pasha.

More than three thousand years ago my ancient ancestors, the Israelites, lived on both sides of the Jordan River. They understood that being divided made them vulnerable to their enemies. They approached the prophet Samuel and asked him to find a man who could unite them and serve as their king. At first, Samuel objected, warning them of the ills of a monarchy, but the people insisted and Saul was anointed first King of Israel.

> And the elders of Israel [said to Samuel]: . . . Now
> make us a king to judge us like all other nations. . . .

And Samuel [said to the people]: This will be the
manner of the king that shall reign over you. He will
take your sons and appoint them for himself, and for
his chariots . . . and make them instruments of war. . . .
    And he will take the tenth of your seed and your
vineyards. . . .
    The people refused to obey the voice of Samuel and
they said: Nay, but we will have a king over us, that we
may be like all other nations, and that our king may
judge us, and go out before us, and fight our battles.

I felt as if I were witnessing the decline of a tribal era
and the dawning of a kingdom, all occuring where the story
of Samuel and the Israelites had taken place. When Abdullah first called upon the Bedouin tribes in 1921 to unite into
one people under his reign, he faced the same apprehension
voiced by Samuel centuries ago — the tribesmen's fear of
conscription, taxation, and subjugation. While the first
decade of Abdullah's reign in Transjordan saw much
progress toward unification, it was also plagued by the in-
surrection of tribes resistant to any form of central authority.

Paradoxically, it was the Transjordanian army, previously shunned by the Bedouin, that played a major role in
the transformation of the tribal society into a twentieth-
century political entity. When Glubb Pasha first took over
the command of the Arab Legion, he decided to build it up
by recruiting Bedouin into its ranks. His superiors doubted
the advisability of this, for they considered the Bedouin illiterate and undisciplined — not the stuff of an efficient
army. It was well known they bowed to no authority, be it
Turkish or British, reserving their allegiance only to their

own tribal chiefs. Glubb was not blind to these problems but nevertheless believed that the Bedouin, if appropriately trained, had the potential of becoming excellent soldiers. He perceived in them what others failed to see — courage, endurance, camaraderie, and a capacity for improvisation. He sat with them night after night around a pit of glowing embers in the open desert, sipping their black coffee. He learned the nuances of their language, observed their customs, admired their love of freedom, expansiveness, and hospitality. The Bedouin in turn became accustomed to Glubb's presence and came to trust him. They included him in their nightly forays deep into the desert.

In time Glubb was able to impress on them that their raids on each other only caused mutual loss of life and property. He also convinced them that, unlike the Turks, Abdullah was their true friend. Had he not defended them from the attacks of the Wahabis? Had he not kept his promise and refrained from coercing their sons to join the military? And above all, was he not a true Bedouin himself, and a descendant of the Prophet Mohammed?

Years of drought, defoliation of the land, shrinking grazing sites, tribal raiding, hunger, and illness, had made the nomadic existence insupportable. Seeking a better future, many young men voluntarily joined Glubb's army, where they learned how to read and write, acquired new vocations, and took on a shared identity.

Abdullah played a central role in the creation of the Arab Legion yet remained relatively peripheral to its operation throughout the mandate period. Although the people of Transjordan made up the rank and file of the military, the chief commander and all the high-ranking officers were

British. The Legion's budget was provided by Whitehall, and it was passed directly on from London to Glubb, not channeled through Abdullah. Information concerning the Legion's operation was often withheld from him, sometimes intentionally and always mindlessly.

I was once commissioned to build a large warehouse for the Arab Legion that involved a sizable area and a large expenditure. When I happened to mention it to Abdullah, I discovered that he knew nothing about the project. I could see his eyes narrow and his fist tighten, but he quickly recovered with a shrug and a smile. Abdullah knew that in the eyes of the British he was mostly a figurehead, useful only for reviewing the troops and handing out medals. But he rarely let his bitterness surface. He was convinced that he could do more for his country through accommodation than by struggling against the powers that be.

As Transjordan developed into a more cohesive entity, and as Abdullah's contribution to the war effort came to be recognized, Britain terminated the mandate and granted the country full political independence. In 1946, twenty-five years to the day after he had entered Transjordan, Abdullah was crowned king of the Hashemite Kingdom of Jordan.

Years later, as I think about the reliance of the Hashemites on the British, I see that this alliance, which facilitated the creation of Jordan, may have been a double-edged sword. Abdullah might not have accomplished his mission without British support, but he came to be perceived as a British collaborator, a man out of touch with the emerging aspirations of his brethren in the region. Abdullah, a leader of the Arab Revolt against Turkey, a man who dreamed of a united Arab nation, was considered a traitor by the more radical forces beginning to make themselves heard in the Arab world. He did not know then that the seeds of his eventual demise were contained within his very success.

I had met the legendary Glubb Pasha on business matters before, though I had never had the chance to spend time with him in a social setting. As I've said, I was often invited to join Abdullah and his Arab sheikhs in storytelling and ballad recitation in Abdullah's tent, located next to Raghdan Palace. But I had never been a guest at his gatherings with British officials. Abdullah knew that the British viewed close relations between Transjordan and the Jewish community of Palestine with disfavor, and that they were perturbed by the business connections between Abdullah and me. Not until the outbreak of the Second World War did the British begin to encourage cooperation between Transjordan and the Jews. It was of course to England's advantage to have us work together in its war effort in the Middle East.

As I entered the tent that evening I was surprised to see that all the guests were British, and I expected stilted manners and formal conversation. I soon discovered that Abdullah's British friends were swept up in the Bedouin mystique, dazzled by a world peopled by nomads roaming freely across the vast desert. Brigadier Glubb was among the distinguished guests, so I knew the evening would be filled with Bedouin stories. He recounted them with no less fervency than a tribal sheikh. This was one he told:

"The famous Sheikh Tafik had a beautiful daughter, but when it came time for her to marry, her father could not find a man to her liking. The girl swore that she would marry only the bravest, the most generous, the most charming sheikh among the Bedouin.

"'There is just one Sheikh who fits that description,' whispered her grandmother to her, 'and it is Sheikh Ibn Humaid. But alas, he is an enemy of our people. Your father and the other sheikhs vowed to sacrifice a camel in celebration when they capture Ibn Humaid.'

"The girl became obsessed with Ibn Humaid, the enemy of her tribe, though she had never set eyes on him.

"Word reached Ibn Humaid about the girl's yearning, and he determined to meet her. He left his tent and rode alone for several days and nights until he reached the enemy camp. Under cover of night he crawled into the tent of Sheikh Tafik, found the daughter's compartment, and spent the night with her.

"In the morning the daughter called to her father from inside her tent:

"'Father, if I only had one request, would you grant it?'

"'It is granted, my favorite daughter. What do you want?'

"'Do you promise?' asked the daughter.

"'I promise,' replied the sheikh.

"'I want you to accept Ibn Humaid as your personal guest.' And with that the daughter stepped out of the tent with her young sheikh.

"Sheikh Tafik jumped to his feet, ready to attack the intruder, but his daughter interceded and reminded her father of his promise. Ibn Humaid was treated with great honor. Several camels were slaughtered for the wedding feast, and the enmity between the two warring tribes ceased forever."

A storyteller would often end his tale with a ballad. Glubb Pasha told a story about the unhappy wife of Caliph Muaja. She had left her parents' tent in the desert to live in the city of Damascus, in a palace surrounded by comfort and luxury, but she longed for her tent and her people. In Arabic Glubb recited a ballad about her. Years later I discovered that he had translated it into English. Here is part of the ballad:

> A tent with rustling breezes cool
> Delights me more than palace high,
> And more the cloak of simple wool
> Than robes in which I learned to sigh.
>
> The crust I ate beside my tent
> Was more than this fine bread to me;
> The wind's voice where the hill path went
> Was more than tambourine can be.

That evening in Abdullah's tent, one story followed another, all told by British officers clearly enamored of a world that celebrated self-sacrifice, hospitality, and the sacredness of promises made. They looked a little odd in their pressed army uniforms and kaffiyehs.

Although he must have heard the stories many times before, Abdullah listened patiently while the Englishmen struggled to pronounce the guttural sounds of the Arabic language. Suddenly I heard him address me. *"Khawaja muhandes,"* he called with a mischievous smile, "it is now your turn to tell a story."

A story? The British immersion in Bedouin tales was not my cup of tea, and for a moment I was at a complete loss. My mind raced helplessly, and then suddenly I had it.

I often wished to tell Abdullah of my respect for his wise leadership and my appreciation for his efforts to achieve peace in the region, but I was reluctant to do so, thinking that he would take it as self-serving flattery. This was my opportunity.

"There was once an effendi," I began, "who owned a large piece of land. He died suddenly, without having told his two sons how the land was to be divided between them after his death. The older son argued that he was entitled to a larger share, by virtue of being the eldest. The younger son claimed that he should receive the larger share, because he had been the one who had tilled the land and made it fertile. The brothers' disagreement turned into a fist fight.

"A Bedouin sheikh rode by on his camel, and when he saw them fighting, he yelled out, 'I will tell you what is right if you stop for a moment.' Surprised, the boys stopped fighting and watched while the sheikh dismounted from his camel and stretched out on the ground. Then he began to laugh heartily, leaving the brothers perplexed.

"'Tell us why you are laughing,' they demanded.

"'I'm listening to the earth laughing!' he replied. 'It is laughing at you. You each believe that a larger share of the land belongs to you, but the earth says that you belong to it.' The sheikh continued to laugh and the brothers joined in. They laughed so hard that they began to feel the earth shake beneath them. The sheikh rode away on his camel, and the brothers returned to their house, in peace."

The king looked at me and gave me a knowing nod of

his head. It was time for him to tell the final story of the evening.

"When Sheikh Ibn Dabi was defeated in battle, his enemies looted everything he possessed. His camels, sheep, the tent with its rugs and utensils — all were taken. A neighbor lent him two camels to take his wife and children to a new location. The sheikh and his family rode for a number of days until they spotted the tent of Mohammed ibn Munaizil. When Mohammed heard their story he knew there was only one thing to be done. He disappeared into the tent and told his wife to prepare a meal for the guests. A sheep was slaughtered and served with rice, bread, and milk. And when the meal was over, the host and his wife and children mounted their camels and rode into the night, leaving their tent and all their belongings to their guests."

Glubb and the British officers knew that they had heard a story none of them could top. It was time to leave.

17

The Last Chess Game

As my friendship with Abdullah grew, so did my puzzlement over its oddity. During our ten years together, we had spent many pleasant hours, drinking aromatic coffee, playing chess, comparing stories of the Bible and the Koran, and reciting poems and ballads, but I never forgot that our basic political views were worlds apart. Our relationship may have survived because we avoided an open discussion of emotionally charged issues rooted in ancient rivalries, leaving the unspoken unspoken.

Still, I wondered if a deeper hostility was yet to surface. While we were carrying on friendly conversations on esoteric subjects, Jews were being exterminated in Nazi camps because their escape route to Palestine was blocked, in no small measure due to Abdullah's influence. I was well aware of the letters he had written to the high commissioners of Palestine, expressing unyielding opposition to the establishment of a national homeland for Jews, and of his alarm over the rapid progress of this development. I was sitting with a man who was playing a significant role in denying the aspirations of my people — and admiring his quick intelligence, warmth, and openness. He was a friend to me, though no friend to my people.

One night while we were playing chess, our cordial discourse moved onto hazardous ground. Selecting his favorite chess set, Abdullah proceeded to place the pieces on the board in a slow and deliberate fashion. The board was made of white and black marble squares and framed with a silver rim. The figures represented an array of modern weapons, including tanks, troop carriers, guns, cannons, and mines. I used to cringe a bit every time he used that set.

Playing with Abdullah required the utmost concentration and tact. He didn't like to be defeated, but he also abhorred winning when his opponent deliberately let him. Since I liked to win as much as he did, I was not inclined to make a consciously wrong move. Fortunately, Abdullah was an excellent player and often won on his own. But when on occasion I happened to score, he would feign anger, muttering displeasure under his breath, while conceding his appreciation with a half-smile.

That night Abdullah won the first game. He pushed all the pieces to my side and said, "See? This is what will happen to your people if I decide to turn my army loose on you."

"And why would you want to do that?" I asked.

"I don't want to, but I may have to," he replied.

"This is the first time I hear you speak like that, *ya sayidi!* What has changed?"

"That's exactly it. It's because nothing has changed." He went on to explain, "I am your friend. You will get nowhere with the Arabs of Palestine. They are your enemies. The mufti is a dangerous man, and together we must get rid of him at all costs and as rapidly as possible."

"But you know, *ya sayidi*, that it wasn't the Jews who stopped you from making peace. It was all the other Arab countries who stood in your way," I protested.

"Yes and no," he replied. "They will always object. They and our British friends don't want to see the Hashemites gain power. The Saudis want a piece of the pie, and so do the Egyptians and the Syrians. But your people need me as much as I need them, and they keep rejecting my offers."

Abdullah was referring to his proposal for a Semitic Kingdom, which intermittently he kept presenting throughout his thirty-year reign. The proposal involved the unification of Palestine and Transjordan into one Hashemite kingdom, the establishment of a Jewish administration in a small area of Palestine, restriction of Jewish immigration, and the prohibition of the sale of Arab land to Jews. As Abdullah put it, "Palestine is one unit. The division between Palestine and Transjordan is artificial. We, Arabs and Jews, can come to terms and live together in peace in the whole country." It was a proposal adamantly rejected by my people, who sought the establishment of their independence in their own homeland.

Whereas I was familiar with Abdullah's position on the question of Palestine, I doubted that he knew much about mine. It occurred to me that it was time for him to know whence I came.

"*Ya sayidi*," I began, "let me tell you a little about the way things look to the other side, to me and my family. My grandparents left Europe in 1880 to go to Palestine with the first organized wave of immigrants. They gave up a relatively comfortable living to work as farmers and artisans in the new land. My parents were among the first to live outside the walls of the Old City of Jerusalem, to build new neighborhoods in a new Jerusalem. You may have seen those plaques that say, 'If I forget thee, O Jerusalem, my right hand shall lose its cunning.' They always hung on the walls of our house."

He was listening. I went on. "The Old City, so holy to you and your people, had been sacred to my people as well and has been my home. I used to walk to school there every day, three miles each direction, and learned the stories of Abraham and Isaac, Joseph and Moses, David and Solomon, stories that took place in the very place where I grew up." The mention of the Biblical figures, familiar to him through the Koran, drew his attention. He nodded with a smile of recognition.

When I spoke about my people's commitment to working on the land, and the change from their faith in the Messiah to self-reliance, he replied, "Yes, yes. That's what I want to see here. Our people talk, talk, talk. But when it comes to doing something about it, it's always *'taal bukra'* — come tomorrow. I wish we could take a little of what you people have."

He was obviously reacting with his own interests in mind, and I wasn't sure he was hearing my point. I tried to articulate it once more. "You see, *ya sayidi*, we want for ourselves what you want for your people. Our people never really left Israel. They were driven away, but never forgot it and never gave up wishing to return. Now that it looks like we are close, we are not willing to settle for being part of a

Semitic Kingdom. We want our own independent state. The same thing that happened to you happened to us. Your family lost the Hejaz to the Saudis, just as we lost our land. Now you are building a new home for the Hashemites here just as we are building a home for our people in Palestine."

Enough said. I was certain that he had heard my arguments many times over, spoken by men of greater authority and power. I knew that my arguments would not change him. But I had to let the truth be spoken between us. With a slight hoarseness in his voice he said, "I am getting older, and after I'm gone you will have no one left to negotiate with." And that was the end of our frank discussion that night. Abdullah was obviously worn out. He got up and disappeared behind the curtain that separated the public and the private areas of the tent.

I walked back to the Philadelphia Hotel. A sliver of moon lit the unpaved path. Amman was sound asleep, and the only sound I heard was that of the pebbles under my feet. I thought about the chess game, of what was said — and what was not. There was much more I had wanted him to know about me and my people, but I couldn't burden him with all of it, not in one night. There would be another chance.

Our discussion must have resembled other encounters between Abdullah and leaders of the Jewish community, both stating their positions and failing to reach a solution, each side trying to understand the other but unable to give up its basic tenets. Did the negotiations with the Jewish leaders also end up in his retreating behind a curtain, whether literal or metaphorical? Abdullah and the Jewish community were at an impasse. Abdullah could not give up his ambition to rule over a unified Transjordan and Palestine, and we could not give up our hope for an independent national home in Palestine. And that is where the pieces stood.

I settled into my comfortable bed for the night but couldn't find sleep. I had noticed lately that Abdullah was showing signs of fatigue. His body was beginning to stoop and the twinkle in his eye was dimming, along with his eyesight. His Bedouin spirits seemed dampened. His ambition to break beyond the borders of his Godforsaken country into Syria and Palestine was totally frustrated and the Zionist movement was showing no sign of yielding to his cravings. But perhaps more important, he was trapped by his own ambivalence, his inability to choose between his desire to expand and his longing for peace. The choice was not long in coming.

The year was 1947. Tensions between the Jewish and Arab communities in Palestine reached a boiling point following the recommendation of a United Nations commission to divide Palestine into two states — Jewish and Arab. Arab armies outside Palestine were ready to invade if a Jewish state was declared. Bands of Palestinian Arabs were roaming the countryside, attacking Jewish settlements, setting up roadblocks, and ambushing vehicles.

My wife was urging me to give up my work in Amman and to return to Jerusalem for good. She feared for my life. But I was not worried. I felt safe among my Arab friends and confident of the protection of the king.

Still, I was aware of noticeable changes taking place around the court. The pitch of the war rhetoric from the

Arab nations was rising across the Middle East, and Abdullah was joining in, though in a somewhat less frenzied tone. Whenever I saw him, he was surrounded by a group of people. Bodyguards? I wondered. I knew that Abdullah normally rejected being crowded by security police and preferred to move around without protection.

Abdullah's attitude toward me was also changing. He no longer stopped to chat with me, or waved when he saw me. We no longer played chess. Had I possibly offended him in some way? Was this his reaction to my earlier frankness? Or was he too preoccupied to attend to personal niceties? Other people at the court were also acting with greater discretion toward me; they were keeping their distance.

I met Mohammed Zubati on his way to the palace. "A lot seems to be going on," I commented.

"It's like sand covering the tents in the storm," he said to me. "The troubles in Palestine may soon reach our corner. Who can stop them?" His words were cryptic yet also a clear signal of danger.

I decided to drop by and see Suliman, who invariably had his finger on the pulse of Amman and felt no compunctions about sharing his views and information with me.

I found him in his garage, tinkering with his car. He slid out from under the chassis, wiped his greasy hands, and greeted me with a wide smile. "Now the car is in good shape. I was just about ready to come and pay you a visit," he said casually.

"Abu Salim, what's going on?" I asked.

"Walls have ears," he replied. "Let's go inside and talk." He took me to the back room of the house and spoke in a low voice. "There's more trouble here than you think. Let's go to the hotel, pick up your things, and get you out of here. I'll tell you more in the car."

I didn't ask questions. Back at the hotel I called my brother, who was working on a project in Shuneh, and insisted that he leave immediately. He told me that Abdullah had already approached him and told him to leave without delay due to the rapid deterioration of the situation.

A few miles out of Amman, Suliman began to talk. I held my breath.

"*Ya aziz*," he said — my dear friend — "things are going to blow up any minute. Did you notice the goings-on around the court? Have you ever seen all those people coming and going? And did you notice how nervous and pale Sayidna has been lately? Bad things are happening. I heard through the grapevine that delegations have been coming from your country and that a lot of meetings are being held here and in Shuneh. I think it was that *yahud* Danin and his people who have been here. Some say that an important Jewish woman came with him. Would you believe it? And Sayidna, he looks so bad. Allah watch over him! They say that Sayidna is very nervous about these meetings. The other Arabs don't approve of his talks with the Jews, and I even heard rumors of threats on his life if he negotiated with your people. You need to know, *ya aziz*, that your life is in danger."

"Why is that?" I asked, trying to appear calm.

He told me that he had been approached by a group of Palestinians belonging to the Freedom Fighters who were roaming the country and carrying out acts of terror. They offered him fifty lira as a reward for delivering me into their hands.

"I refused the offer," he said, "because of my loyalty to Sayidna and my gratitude to you, Khawaja Cohen."

When we reached my home in Jerusalem, I asked him to come in and join us for supper, but he refused. I understood his reluctance. He would not hand me over as a hostage, but he could not put himself and his family in jeopardy by maintaining close contact with the enemy. As he was getting back into his car, he waved. "As my people say, all good things come to an end, but *Inshallah* we will meet again."

This was the last I saw of Suliman, or of King Abdullah. Years of construction came to an end. Years of war and destruction were about to begin.

18

Friend Turns Foe

THE THREAT OF WAR WAS LOOMING when the United Nations Special Commission on Palestine (UNSCOP) completed its report. As predicted, it recommended the partition of Palestine into two independent states. The part allotted for the Jewish state was no larger than New Jersey, but the recommendation was readily embraced by the Jewish people, for it gave them their age-old dream of a free nation in their ancient land.

For most Arabs in the Middle East, the very notion of a Jewish state, no matter how small, was anathema. Angry voices rose across the region, threatening obliteration of the state if the UNSCOP recommendations were implemented. Threats of war were being broadcast daily on the Arab radio and from microphones placed on the tops of minarets. Acts of violence by local Arab gangs were increasing, and roaming irregular armies were gaining in number. They bombed residential neighborhoods, burned commercial establishments, attacked vehicles, and inflicted heavy casualties. The clouds of war were gathered.

As the final vote on the partition plan neared, we were

filled with an odd mixture of joy and gloom, the realization of our dream marred by the dread of war.

The General Assembly convened on November 29, 1947, to act on the recommendation for partition. Thousands gathered in the court of the Jewish Agency in Jerusalem to hear the results of the vote. Loudspeakers were placed in the plaza to announce the roll call as it came in from Lake Success, New York. "Afghanistan — no" was the first to pierce the total silence, followed by "Australia — yes," "Belgium — yes," and so on down the alphabet: "France — *oui*," "United Kingdom — abstain," "Union of Soviet Socialist Republics — yes," "United States of America — yes." The roll call ended with Yugoslavia's abstention. With the thump of a gavel came the historic statement, loud and clear: "Thirty-three in favor, thirteen against, ten abstentions, one absent. The resolution is adopted."

Few waited to hear the aftermath of the vote. People were cheering, singing, and dancing in the streets of Jerusalem until dawn. But the next morning's newspapers cut short the jubilation. The headlines celebrated the birth of the new nation with bold letters: THE STATE OF ISRAEL IS BORN. LONG LIVE ISRAEL. Beneath the headline read: "Arab Delegates Threaten War." The Arab representatives had walked out of the United Nations in protest, proclaiming: "The partition line will be little more than a line of fire and blood."

The termination of the British mandate in Palestine and the evacuation of British forces were due to occur in six months. Britain was determined to pull out, whatever happened. Jews and Arabs were already fighting an undeclared war. We kept hoping that Jordan and the Arab Legion would stay out of the war, for Abdullah was the most moderate Arab neighbor and the one whose rhetoric against the Jews was least inflammatory. But more important, he had a vested interest in peace with Israel. On several occasions he had indicated his readiness to discuss a new partition plan with Israel. Under his plan the Jewish state would be established in the part allotted by the UN, and Abdullah would integrate with Jordan (annex, essentially) the Arab part, thus expanding the boundaries of his small country. To do this he needed the passive consent of the Jewish leadership.

I had no doubt of Abdullah's peaceful intentions. He was a man who always sought accommodation and compromise, who remained open to new ideas and possibilities. I could not believe that he would lead his army in war against us, nor that a pragmatist who always preferred diplomacy to war would take up arms. I was delighted to hear that a decision was made to send a Jewish representative to meet with Abdullah and explore further options for peaceful coexistence.

Years later I learned that in November 1947 a meeting had been held between King Abdullah and Golda Meir, whose straight talk and unpretentious manners earned her much affection and admiration. She was generally referred to simply as "Golda." The meeting was held on the border between Jordan and Israel, in a place called Naharayim, the site of the first electrical power station in Israel and a source of electrical power for Abdullah and his court. Mohammad Zubati had driven Golda to the Jordanian border. They were accompanied by an Israeli named Ezra Danin, an expert in Middle Eastern affairs and a friend of King Abdullah, who served as interpreter.

At first Abdullah was chagrined at having to conduct political business with a woman. He considered women inferior to men and did not believe that they belonged in politics. But his personal feelings did not keep him from working with her toward a peaceful solution to the conflict.

Abdullah and Meir were able to reach a tentative understanding. Jordan would refrain from attacking Israel and deny Iraqi forces access to the Israeli border. In return, Israel would refrain from interfering with Abdullah's move to annex the Arab part of the partitioned Palestine. The agreement was not formalized, but Abdullah assured Meir that as a Bedouin, he would never break a promise to a neighbor, nor lie to a woman.

The agreement would have held major advantages for Israel. The Arab Legion, the most effective and best-trained Arab army in the Middle East, would have been neutralized, and the Iraqi army prevented from reaching Israel's border.

Despite his goodwill and poetic promises, Abdullah's position was shifting. Before the proclamation of the State of Israel in May 1948, it became evident that the king was planning to join the other Arab nations in war against Israel. A day before the war, Mrs. Meir went to meet Abdullah again.

Abdullah was reluctant to hold the meeting, knowing that if word got out it would weaken his standing in the Arab world, but was persuaded otherwise. Zubati offered his own winter house in Shuneh as a meeting place.

Meir was in Jerusalem at the time and couldn't get out, because the roads surrounding the city had been blocked. She was flown out of Jerusalem to Haifa in a single-engine plane along with her assistant Ezra Danin. They were to meet Zubati in Naharayim and be driven to Jordan.

On the way to the border, Danin expressed doubt that anything would come out of that highly dangerous journey. "Why are you doing this?" he asked.

Golda responded: "I am willing to try anything if I can save the life of only one Israeli soldier."

In Naharayim, Golda and Danin donned their disguises. For Golda it was the voluminous black dress of an Arab woman, and for Danin traditional Arab headgear. Driven by Zubati in an official royal car, they were waved over the bridge into Jordan.

The visitors were received graciously by Zubati's Syrian wife. Golda barely touched her sumptuous lunch; she was too nervous to eat. Despite the tension, the women managed a casual chat. Mrs. Zubati, who had been an English teacher before her marriage, lamented the fate of educated Arab women, who were relegated to insignificant duties.

"And I long for such a time when I would be totally bored," replied Golda.

Abdullah joined them, looking depressed and withdrawn.

"Have you broken your promise?" asked Golda in her straightforward manner.

Abdullah explained that he could not betray his Arab allies. However, he was willing to make another effort to dissuade his brethren from declaring war, if Israel agreed to "postpone" its declaration of independence. "What is the big hurry?" he asked. "You need to be patient."

"We have been waiting for over two thousand years," Golda responded. "You can hardly call this impatient."

Abdullah presented his final offer, a variation on the same Semitic Kingdom proposal he had articulated at various times in the past. Israel would be granted a small region administered by the Jews as an autonomous entity, and given representation in parliament under the sovereignty of the Hashemite Kingdom. The proposal was clearly unacceptable. It had been rejected by the Jewish community in the past, and was all the more unacceptable now that the right of the Jewish people to their ancient patrimony had been confirmed by the international body of nations. It was obvious that Abdullah had already made up his mind. He knew that his proposal would never be accepted, and was prepared for the rejection and its aftermath.

As the meeting was about to adjourn, Abdullah said to his friend Danin: "I am very sorry it turned out this way. It would be a shame to shed blood and cause destruction. Let us hope that we shall not break off the contact between us."

Danin hesitated for a moment to make one last comment. He implored the king to be cautious. The custom of people approaching him to kiss the hem of his robe greatly endangered his safety, said Danin. With a resigned smile Abdullah responded: "I would never stop my people from showing their devotion. And as to my safety, let Fate take care of that."

Zubati appeared stunned by the outcome. Defending his monarch's stance, he said that Abdullah was caught in a web he could not escape. Under heavy pressure from his

Arab brethren, he had no alternative. "If Abdullah had a choice between a room full of gold and peace, he would undoubtedly choose peace." But Zubati, for all his goodwill, did not wish to transport Meir and Danin back to Israel. Instead he ordered a chauffeur to drive them back to Naharayim. It was a dangerous trip. Iraqi soldiers were already patrolling the area. The driver lost his nerve and dropped his passengers a few miles short of their destination. Golda and Danin managed to make it the rest of the way on foot.

The State of Israel was proclaimed on May 14, 1948. Abdullah was declared chief commander of the Arab armies. Standing in the middle of the Allenby Bridge, a revolver in his hand, he fired the first shot to signify the beginning of the war. That same day the Egyptian army crossed into the Negev Desert, the Iraqis moved toward the Jordan River, Syrian forces attacked Israeli villages in the Galilee, and the Jordanians crossed the Jordan River. It was the beginning of the war the Israelis call the War of Independence, and the Arabs the War of Defeat and Destruction.

Within a few days, batteries of the Arab Legion were bombarding Jerusalem. A shell fell near my house, causing windowpanes to shake and break. A picture I had constructed over ten years began to shatter like the windows around me.

In May 1948 the Old City of Jerusalem fell to the Jordanians. The Arab Legion entered the Jewish Quarter, destroyed its synagogues, desecrated the Jewish cemetery, and took the men prisoner. Roads connecting the city to the rest of the country were blocked. New Jerusalem was also under siege, bombarded relentlessly by Abdullah's forces positioned on the hills. Food and water were scarce, and people standing in line for their rations were often hit by bullets and shrapnel.

My older son was fighting the Egyptians in the Negev. My wife, her parents, and our twelve-year-old son moved into the cellar. They used to come out when there was a lull and use the meager supply of water left after bathing to water some vegetables, and give part of their bread rations to feed the few hens strolling in the yard. It kept us from feeling perpetually hungry.

Barring a direct hit, my family was relatively safe, though frightened out of their wits by every missile shrieking overhead. I could not stay cooped up in the cellar. In spite of my wife's admonition, I preferred to sleep upstairs, trying to ignore the explosions and the gaping holes in the walls. I lost my sense of reality; my world had been turned upside down.

I knew that the military machine was already in motion. But a part of me refused to accept this. I could not believe that the smiling, gracious man who had repeatedly proclaimed his peace-loving intentions would lead his people and mine to destruction. I was angry, angry at my friend, angry at my own blindness, angry at my failure to recognize the truth about him — too angry to wait for the war to end. I decided to enlist in the Israeli Defense Force.

The recruitment officers were not impressed with my application. I was over fifty, overweight, and not particularly fit. My only military experience had been at a Turkish army training camp thirty years earlier. They must have thought that I would be a greater liability than an asset, and politely suggested that I return home until they found something useful for me to do. A few days later I was surprised to receive an order to appear at the barracks in south Jerusalem. I had been assigned to the military police to act as a judge of the military court.

A few days in the courtroom made it obvious to me that meting out punishment to soldiers who violated furlough was not my idea of fighting a war. I couldn't help thinking that the young men I saw might be injured or taken captive the next day, and found passing judgment on them difficult. Within a short time, however, I was presented with an opportunity to volunteer for a most unusual mission — the crossing of the Valley of Damnation.

Across from Mount Zion, on another hill, is Yemin Moshe, the first Jewish community to be built outside the wall at the end of the last century. Between the two hills lies the Valley of Hinnom, home to a small Arab village. Fertile gardens and fields are tilled by hand on neatly leveled terraces, where grow fruits and vegetables. The olive trees in the valley are among the oldest in Jerusalem — some are thousands of years old. Stone and mud houses hug the side of the hill; the paths between them are covered with mud in the winter and dust in summer. It looks like a place where people live in peace and tranquillity. But this valley has seen horror. In Biblical times it was known as the "inferno," a gehenna, where boys and girls were thrown onto burning altars as sacrifices to the god Moloch. The sound of trumpets, cymbals, and drums drowned the shrieks of dying children. Young Israeli soldiers had also died in the Valley of Damnation.

A small garrison was stationed outside the wall on the southwestern side of Mount Zion. The troops, camouflaged against Arab snipers shooting from the towers of the Old City, were preparing to break through one of the gates into the Old City and retake it. They were being supplied with food and ammunition by way of the Valley of Hinnom. Arab snipers would aim at the Israelis crossing the valley, however, so few supplies were able to reach the garrison. The number of casualties was mounting.

A new approach was being contemplated: a cable car between the two hillsides, operated in total darkness. When it was ready to be tested, a few noncombat recruits were called in and offered the chance to volunteer for a dangerous mission. Only after I had volunteered did I learn that I was to board a cable car at 11:00 P.M., taking with me a barrel of explosives, munitions, and some food and medical supplies. My job was to cross the Valley of Hinnom, assess the level of noise emitted by the pulleys and cogs, and make contact with the garrison stationed on the side of the hill. I was to help unload the car and then return.

The car glided smoothly over the cables. Except for the sound of wailing coyotes in the valley below and the occasional burst of gunfire, the ride was eerily quiet, almost enjoyable in a strange way. I was surprised at how calm I felt. It must have been the spirit of my grandfather Avram Itzhak helping me maintain my equanimity.

My grandfather had given up his study bench in a yeshiva in Lithuania to come to Israel and become a farmer. However, during the off-season he used to spend time poring over the holy books in the synagogue. One day while he was so engaged, a fire broke out and moved rapidly toward the synagogue. Neighbors ran to warn him, but Avram Itzhak wouldn't budge. He was certain that no harm would befall him so long as he was sitting in a place of prayer. The fire progressed rapidly, but when it reached the door of the synagogue it died. The story of my grandfather's spirit had often served me well. It had also betrayed me. I felt a slight shiver when I remembered the time I failed to insure my factory for fire damage, believing that the fire would die out at the door — only to be proven wrong.

Five young men were waiting for me at the landing on Mount Zion. They quickly unloaded the supplies and sent me back by way of the primitive sky trolley. It was past midnight, and the air was crisp as I moved slowly above the Valley of Damnation. For some reason, I was thinking of Abdullah. Was he my friend? My enemy? A good man? An evil man? In the confusion of war, no label seemed to fit.

After taking the Old City and part of the west bank of the river, the Arab armies began losing ground. During a short cease-fire Abdullah began negotiating with Israel again. His kingdom having expanded, Abdullah was seeking peace with the Jews. He was being threatened by other Arab nations, who did not view his expansion with favor. He was also being challenged by the indigenous Palestinian population, led by extreme nationalists. He needed a quiet border along the long Jordan River and access to the sea through Israel. But for all his attempts at reconciliation and cooperation, he never seemed able to finalize a deal. He wavered between approaching an agreement and withdrawing from it, making promises and then breaking them. Ben-Gurion, Israel's first prime minister, began to lose faith in Abdullah. As he put it, the old man had good intentions but couldn't deliver the goods.

As I followed Abdullah's brinkmanship politics, I began

to understand more fully what I had understood only vaguely during my stay in Amman. Abdullah was neither hawk nor dove, neither friend nor foe. He was a man driven by conflicting forces. And they were taking their toll on him. As he was approaching the end of his life, his inner strength was growing brittle and vulnerable to pressure.

The Israelis found his proposals too extreme and uncompromising. The Arabs saw his position as too lenient and compromising; the more militant even referred to him as a traitor. His ambition to be the spiritual and political leader of the Arab world never left him, but his position of leadership among the Arabs was weakening because of his willingness to consider peace with Israel. His ambition to expand his borders was realized, but the Palestinian Arabs who came under his jurisdiction were seeking their own self-determination. His decision to open the doors to Palestinian refugees was backfiring, because their numbers were changing the nature of the population and with it the composition of the governing bodies. Bringing these forces into harmony was beyond his powers, as it would have been for any politician. He was caught in a web of complexities and contradictions: love and hurt, hope and disappointment, caution and ambition, soaring idealism and pragmatism — friend and foe. His smile was genuine, not a mask. Only a light veil over a king's grief.

19

Ezekiel's Vision

As I write this, it is now three years since the end of the 1948 war. We are still rebuilding our homes, replanting scorched fields, and rebuilding bridges. Those who survived the war live with the painful realization that thousands of young men and women who lost their lives on the battlefield can never share in the recovery. Even now, three years later, I feel pangs of anxiety upon meeting an acquaintance I have not seen since the end of the war, lest I hear of a tragedy.

As we mourn our losses, the slow process of healing begins. And as the people of Israel undertake the creation of a safe haven for Jews seeking refuge in the ancient land of their forefathers, there is growing optimism in the air. Israel survived the attack of five Arab armies. Its independence, won through fire and blood, is fully attained. It is as if the words of the prophet Ezekiel, spoken thousands of years ago, have come to be.

> The hand of the Lord was upon me and set me down in the midst of the valley which was full of bones. . . .
> And he said unto me, Son of Man, can these bones live? . . .

. . . Prophesy upon these bones and say unto them: . . .
"I will . . . bring flesh upon you and cover you with skin
and put the spirit into you, and you shall live; . . ."
. . . and the spirit came into them, and they lived,
and they stood upon their feet.

And here they are, the discarded remnants of humanity, skin and bones, arriving on our shores. Boats full of immigrants are docking at our ports, filled with people who survived the Holocaust only to be interned in DP (displaced person) camps because no country would admit them. Wearing their tattered clothes, identification numbers tattooed on their wrists, without a soul to call their kin, they are embraced by strangers. Wave after wave, the beaten men and women walking down the gangplanks of dilapidated vessels breathe new life, learn Hebrew, engage in gainful occupations, and begin to establish new families. No longer nameless, they are now citizens.

The refugees, each group with its unique language, dress, and customs, create an air of excitement and challenge, for we are trying to mold a new nation out of a sea of human diversity — 25,000 from British detention camps in Cyprus; 70,000 from camps in Germany, Austria, and Italy; 104,000 from Poland; 119,000 from Romania; 30,000 from Bulgaria; 50,000 from Yemen; 130,000 from Iraq. Also Jews from distant Kuchin in India, old communities from Iran, Syria, and Egypt — altogether 730,000 men, women, and children arriving from all corners of the globe and absorbed by Israel. The small Israeli population, numbering around 600,000, has more than doubled in the course of the last three years.

Among the immigrants I had employed in my business was one who left a deep impression on me. He was Yehye (a name that means "he shall live"), a Yemenite Jew of indeterminate age who came to work for me as a night watchman. Dressed in an ankle-length shirt and a pointed skullcap, his dark narrow face adorned by a beard and side curls, he looked anxious and forlorn. I soon discovered, however, that he was a learned student of the Bible and a skilled artisan. In Yemen he had worked as a jewelry silversmith, one of the few occupations Jews were permitted to hold. He and his family had lived in a segregated community, under the constant shadow of persecution and religious discrimination. When Yehye and his brethren heard of the establishment of Israel, they were determined to come here and await the Messiah. In 1949 Yehye and almost the entire Jewish community moved on foot to the British colony of Aden, located at the tip of the Arabian Peninsula, where they were met by Israel's newly established El-Al Airline and flown to Israel. The massive airlift was to remain in the annals of Israel as the "flight of the magic carpet."

I came to know Yehye better while we sat together outside my factory on cold winter nights. I occasionally dropped in to check on him, for I had noticed that Yehye liked to indulge in generous sips of arak, a potent alcoholic drink, and I wondered if he would fall asleep while on watch. Most nights, however, I found him alert and eager to share his drink. After a few swigs of arak, our chilled bones would warm a bit and Yehye would lose his reserve and pour out his heart, complaining about the hardships in the new land. Government officials meant well but didn't understand that there were tensions between different immigrant groups in the camp where he lived, and a scarcity of food and money. Yehye was particularly perturbed at the large number of young secular Israeli men who wore no skullcaps and ignored religious customs in the very heart of the holy city of Jerusalem. To my question of whether he regretted coming such a long way to encounter such disappointments, he responded, "Not for a minute! I will never forget how I used to get off the road when a Muslim passed by, and when I had to sell my wares below cost because the thugs in the market would force me to do so, topping their robbery with curses and mockery. And when my children needed a Hebrew book, I had to search for days and pay a whole month's wages to get one. No, God forbid, no regrets!"

Yehye once invited me to his home and I accepted willingly. I found his tent among hundreds of other military tents provided by the Israeli government for new immigrants. The immigrant camp called Ma'abarah ("transitional place") was erected as a temporary measure, but Yehye as well as many other immigrants could not be moved to permanent housing for some time, because construction was not keeping pace with the new immigration. The family tent contained three iron beds shared by Yehye, his wife, and five sons. A table, two chairs, a kerosene lamp, a few hooks to hang their clothes, and a box for utensils completed the household furnishings. Cooking was done outside on a stove fueled by coal or wood. I was surprised to see a flower and vegetable garden growing around the tent, carefully tended by Yehye's wife and his children.

Yehye pulled a box from the corner of the tent and took out a few pieces of jewelry, which he laid out on a bed. They were pieces he had crafted for his wife to wear at their wedding in Yemen. Among them was a necklace consisting of a heavy silver chain with small silver pendants in the shape of almonds, pomegranates, and bells hanging from it. There were bracelets made of twisted silver rope and a beautiful headband of embroidered black velvet embossed with silver flowers and colorful beads. Yehye then took out an old Bible he had brought with him from Yemen. He took a pillow off the bed, placed it on the floor, put the Bible on top of it, and called in his children.

Four boys, ranging in age from five to twelve, sat on the floor around the book and proceeded to recite a chapter from Genesis in a loud singsong, rocking their bony bodies back and forth. Like many other Yemenite children, they were able to perform the remarkable feat of reading from a single text from different sides. It was a skill they had acquired because Hebrew books were scarce and a single book had to be shared by several children at one time.

The cantillation of their chant was foreign, but the text was the same I had recited in the heder fifty years ago. And that, I thought, was our big challenge and opportunity: the gathering of diverse Jewish ethnic groups with their own languages and customs who were, nevertheless, part of the same people. We were so different from one another in our ways, and yet we were all using the same language, reading the same Bible, reciting the same prayers, and sharing the same aspirations.

As I bid the family farewell, Yehye said with a wink, "You see, *Adon* Cohen? It's not so bad. After all, these are *hevlei mashiakh*, the pain we must undergo before the coming of the Messiah."

This unique period of challenge and creation has been

a time of personal renewal for me. In the fervor of preparing new land for planting and replacing manual labor with machinery, a large number of orchards had to be uprooted to make room for the mechanized picking equipment. Among them were some ancient olive groves. When I heard of the thousands of discarded olive trees dumped on the roadsides to be burnt, I decided to take a look. Abandoned trunks, some eroded by wind and rain, others coated with a smooth, unharmed layer of bark, each told their own story: of famine and plenty, war and peace, storm and tranquillity. I collected the most convoluted, pitted, and scabrous trunks, thinking they would contain the most intricate patterns of color and grain. I piled them in a vacant lot near my factory to dry in the sun and began to explore their attributes as soon as they were ready. It quickly became evident that the trunks I had selected were too tortured and too brittle to yield pieces of wood large enough for furniture construction. After extensive experimentation, however, I found a way to combine the small pieces into mosaics, patterned in infinite varieties of design, that could be used to make large pieces. Thus began perhaps the most productive period of my life. I was fortunate enough to be able to recruit artists and artisans who were equally taken by the colors of honey, wheat, and amber of this wonderful wood. Together we have produced numerous pieces for homes, stores, and places of worship.

Is the new enterprise merely an accident? Perhaps not. Is this not a time when we are all engaged in the creation of new patterns, piecing together fragments into a larger mosaic?

20

Murder in the Mosque

ABDULLAH HAD FINALLY BROKEN FREE of the borders of his parched land. Victory, power, control, and adulation were no longer just intoxicating dreams. Of the five Arab countries that invaded Israel in 1948, only Jordan emerged undefeated, not only adding the West Bank to its territory but also tripling its population.

His had been a long, arduous road, punctuated by both accomplishments and disappointments. Abdullah had first boarded the Damascus-Hejaz train in 1921, heading northward to seek Hashemite ascendancy in the Middle East, but he never conquered Damascus nor succeeded in leading the Arab nations. Instead he settled in an area east of the Jordan River previously unknown as a political entity, and created a new country. Though formidable, what he had managed to do had fallen short of fulfilling his father's legacy, so deeply etched in his mind and soul. And though his country had achieved political independence, it remained financially and militarily dependent on England. Relations with his Arab neighbors were acrimonious, and his attempts to find common ground with Israel had failed. When I last saw Abdullah, before the war, he had appeared depressed. His formerly spry gait was more tentative, the twinkle in his eye was dimmed, and his back was stooped by the burden of his office.

The war had given him new life and revived his dreams. The realization of Hashemite ambitions was closer now than ever before. The West Bank was annexed to Jordan and the Old City brought into the fold of Islam, and he finally would have won his father's approval — had his father lived long enough to witness his accomplishments. In my mind's eye I could see Abdullah revitalized in body and soul, his steps regaining their rapid clip, his back arching with pride while new vistas appeared on the horizon.

But I wondered whether he saw the deadly pitfalls his success had created. If he did, he kept it to himself. His public statements bespoke a man full of confidence and authority, and I tended to believe that they reflected his true feelings. However, his particular blend of grand ambition and quiet submission to destiny may have rendered him oblivious to the perils around him.

In July 1951, Amman was deeply shaken. The former prime minister of Lebanon, a close friend of Abdullah's, was murdered during his visit to the Jordanian capital. Never before had a political assassination occurred in that peaceful land. The people of Jordan were gripped with anxiety. Palace security, consisting of the most elite and loyal Bedouin and Circassian guards, was doubled, and high government officials stayed close to home. Aware of his plans to visit the West Bank and Jerusalem the following Friday, several of Abdullah's intimates attempted to dissuade him from going to the city, a hotbed of Palestinian opposition to his regime. Refusing to change his mind, Abdullah quoted them an Arab proverb: "Until my day comes nobody can harm me, and when my day comes no one can guard me." But it was more than a fatalism that caused Abdullah to ignore his friends' warnings. He was determined to demonstrate to friend and foe that nothing would make him yield to fear, nor interfere with his ultimate authority.

On the first day of his trip to the West Bank, Abdullah visited villages and conferred with his supporters. Villagers lined the road, cheering enthusiastically and waving Jordanian flags. Pushing forward to touch their leader, the crowd broke through one of the barricades and separated Abdullah from his security guard. Oblivious to the danger, the king stepped out of his car and began to shake hands with them, allowing some to get close enough to kiss the hem of his gown. The crowd shouted, *"Ya Abu Talal, hameena!"* — O father of Talal, protect us! The hills around echoed their cheer while Abdullah's car moved slowly down the road. Reassured by this welcome from people whose support he had always sought, Abdullah proceeded toward Jerusalem.

Abdullah approached the Aqsa mosque, the third most important shrine for Islam and the site of his father's grave, surrounded by the elite Hashemite Regiment led by Colonel Habis Majali, a trusted friend and a descendant of a tribe known for its staunch loyalty to the king. Abdullah was accompanied by his grandson Hussein; other dignitaries had chosen to remain in Amman that day. Thousands lined the streets of the Old City, some waving enthusiastically, some looking disapproving. Noticing some of the grim faces, Abdullah asked in jest, "What is this? A funeral?" Majali and his guards tightened the security ring around the king. "Don't imprison me, *ya Habis!*" Abdullah yelled at the commander of the guard when they reached the mosque. He wished to enter the place of worship unencumbered, confident of Allah's protective shield in the holy shrine. Heeding his command, the military police stepped back and let Abdullah walk ahead. As the old sheikh of the mosque came forward to greet the king and kiss his hand, a young man stepped out from behind the door and shot Abdullah in the head. The king died instantly, falling forward, his turban rolling on the floor.

Hussein was the assassin's next target. The young prince saw a man with clenched teeth and glazed eyes pointing a gun at him and was hurled to the ground by the force of the bullet. Miraculously, he was not hurt. The bullet hit a medal on his uniform, which he had worn that day at his grandfather's insistence. The assassin, standing in plain view, was killed on the spot by the king's guard.

Random shooting and chaos followed in the Old City. Amman was gripped with mourning and fear. The Jewish community in Israel was stunned. The only Arab leader ready to consider coexistence with Israel was gone.

No single event led to Abdullah's assassination, but rather a coalescence of political and personal factors, with Abdullah's attempting to reach peace with Israel at the center of them. In the aftermath of the Arab defeat in the 1948 war, there were internal tensions and instability throughout the region. A revolution toppled the government of Syria; the monarchies of Egypt and Iraq were on the verge of collapse. Jordan, the only Arab victor in the war, became a target of Arab anger. Abdullah was accused of sabotaging Egypt's military offensive during the war, of pursuing expansionist ambitions at the expense of other Arab nations, and of colluding with Britain and Israel. An excerpt from an Egyptian daily provides a typical example of the hostility felt in those days toward Abdullah: "The time has come for the Arab League to cut off relations with Transjordan, the country that betrayed Islam and Arab unity. The time has come to sever this decayed member, bury it, and heap dung over it." The man who had hoped to bring all Arab countries under his wing was shunned, isolated, and threatened.

Trouble had also been brewing within. The population of Jordan, which numbered no more than half a million before the war of 1948, tripled with the influx of refugees from Palestine and with the annexation of the West Bank. Giving Palestinians full rights as Jordanians had led to the rapid growth of a political opposition, formerly nonexistent. Spurred by Abdullah's old antagonist Hajj Amin el-Husseini, the grand mufti of Jerusalem, they vehemently expressed their opposition to the annexation of the West Bank and to Abdullah's overtures of peace to Israel. Abdullah's oncesecure position as an absolute monarch and beloved patriarch was fatally weakened.

Despite his ostracism by the Arab League, the constant attacks by his many opponents, and a growing reluctance among his own ministers to further his peace-seeking efforts, Abdullah continued to conduct secret negotiations with Israel. He realized that his country, whose economy had been drained by the war, literally could no longer afford bloodshed, and that peace held the only promise of revitalizing it. New markets, joint economic projects, access to the Mediterranean Sea, and, above all, quiet along his longest border could only be attained by peace. "I am not a Zionist," he once said. "I simply believe that peace with Israel is in the best interest of the Jordanian people."

Many Palestinians did not share his pragmatism. The assassin was a young Palestinian in his early twenties, a member of the Jihad organization. The discovery of the ownership of the gun led to the arrest of other Palestinian radicals associated with the grand mufti. The man leading the group in Jerusalem, Dr. Musah el-Husseini, was a relative of the mufti. He confessed to the crime, justifying his action on the grounds that the king was a traitor, responsible for the defeat of 1948, and an obstacle to the establishment of an independent Arab Palestine.

Further investigations uncovered a plot led by Abdullah el-Tel, the former military governor of East Jerusalem, who was believed to have masterminded the assassination. When I learned of el-Tel's role in the assassination, an old and familiar echo resonated in my mind. Abdullah el-Tel had been one of the king's favorites, a courageous young officer in the Arab Legion. The king first noticed him during the war of 1948 when he visited the front. El-Tel had given Abdullah a tour of the battleground, and the king was impressed by the energetic major. "You are a capable soldier," he exclaimed. "One day I will promote you to the rank of colonel."

These were not empty words. The king was on the lookout for men like Abdullah el-Tel. It was a time when heavy criticism was being leveled at Abdullah for retaining British officers in command of the Arab Legion. Glubb Pasha was still leading Jordan's national army, and other British officers continued to hold the highest positions. Aware of the need to promote Jordanian leadership in the armed forces, Abdullah had identified el-Tel as a likely candidate for promotion. Glubb Pasha, however, had his reservations. He knew of Abdullah's tendency to put his faith in men who were not always reliable. Indeed, suspicious of el-Tel's loyalty, Glubb warned the king, telling him "the wine of his success had reached his head and intoxicated him." Abdullah ignored Glubb's reservations and appointed el-Tel military governor of East Jerusalem. As Abdullah's confidence in him grew, so did his level of responsibility. The new confidant became the liaison between the king and the Israeli government in the sensitive business of receiving and submitting secret plans for a peace agreement.

Abdullah el-Tel was an ambitious man and prone to self-aggrandizement. When he demanded to be promoted to the rank of brigadier, Glubb flatly refused. This time Abdullah did not push the matter. It is said that el-Tel's anger was so great that he began to conspire against the king, plotting to overthrow the monarchy. He left abruptly for Egypt, carrying with him copies of the secret correspondence between Jordan and Israel. It did not take long for the documents to be published by the Egyptian press in their entirety. Abdullah was branded the enemy of the Arab people and targeted for retaliation. Calls for his murder echoed throughout the Arab world. El-Tel joined the chorus by personally attacking his former benefactor. "The king was a traitor who sold military plans to the Israelis," he said, "and the Arab Legion is an instrument of the British, who prevented it from fighting Israel."

Following the assassination, Abdullah el-Tel was convicted in absentia of conspiracy to commit murder. Egypt refused to extradite him and, unlike the other conspirators, who were executed, his life was spared.

It would be simplistic to attribute King Abdullah's assassination to the betrayal of one man, but it is equally impossible to ignore the personal factors underlying this heinous act. Abdullah generally abhorred empty words of flattery and self-serving platitudes, but he nevertheless often fell victim to the schemes of those who managed to conceal their self-seeking intentions. I think of Mohammed Zubati, the king's confidant, and Nahada, his third wife. To both might be ascribed deviousness and hypocrisy, though of course compared to those of Abdullah el-Tel their manipulations seem relatively harmless, almost childishly innocent.

Abdullah was not blind to the machinations of some of his favorites; he was often well aware of them. But the prankster in him sometimes pretended ignorance, secretly enjoying their games. Furthermore, he was generous and forgiving. If people took advantage of his love and protection, it was of no great consequence, for usually all that was involved was material gain, and this meant little to him. What mattered was devotion and unbending loyalty, which both Zubati and Nahada demonstrated in abundance. But Abdullah had seriously misjudged the nature of el-Tel, who acted like a loving son but was both blindly ambitious and vengeful, willing to serve as an instrument in the hands of political forces in the region.

A braiding of narrow personal vendetta and huge powerful interests, fired by facts and fictions, fanaticism, hatred, and the quest for dominance, brought about Abdullah's death. And in the end remains the paradox, the irony of his life and death — a king whose own achievements were part of his undoing.

My sadness over Abdullah's death does not lessen, even at the end of this quasi-objective narrative about its causes. Students of history may well differ with me over some of the facts, or my interpretation of them. My sadness, however, emanates not only from his loss to me, but from the realization that the same forces of hatred that ended his life continue to rage around us.

21

Who Will Be King?

Tensions between Jordanians and Palestinians intensified upon Abdullah's assassination. Palestinians openly rejoiced. Violent clashes broke out between the Hashemite Regiment and Arabs in the Old City. Plans to bury the king next to his father's grave in Jerusalem were canceled to avert further conflict with Palestinians and to keep inflamed passions in check. There was no funeral procession through the streets of Amman, no public display of grief. Instead, King Abdullah was buried on the palace grounds, following a short procession around the royal compound. The brief interment ceremony was attended by only a select group.

Headed by Tawfik Abul Huda, the king's loyal cabinet, with the support of the army, acted as an interim government and appeared to be running things smoothly — until it came time to resolve the issue of Abdullah's succession. The king had left no clear instructions as to his choice of an heir to his crown. The same confident monarch who had believed that he knew what was best for his country had been in a deep quandary when it came to naming his successor. He had been profoundly disappointed in his eldest son of course. It had become obvious that Talal's illness, eventually diagnosed as schizophrenia, would prevent him from being a suitable occupant of the throne. And Naif's abilities also gave Abdullah pause. He also explored the possibility of forming a confederation with Iraq, to be headed by his nephew King Faisal, though this would have entailed the potential loss of Jordan's sovereignty.

Prince Hussein, Talal's eldest son, was Abdullah's real hope. I well remember the warm relationship they had. Abdullah's face would light up when the young prince came to visit. He would often interrupt important business to greet the boy and show him off. Young Hussein used to visit the palace early in the morning to join his grandfather for a light breakfast of flatbread and coffee flavored with cardamom. Together they would review Hussein's religious studies and engage in long conversations. As Hussein grew older and perfected his English, he often served as his grandfather's interpreter and at times accompanied him on trips abroad.

Hussein was only sixteen when his grandfather was shot, not quite ready for the monarchy. Naif became regent, for Talal was hospitalized in Switzerland. Encouraged by his wife and his following among army officers, Naif was preparing to declare himself king. He was prevented from doing so by Prime Minister Abul Huda, by the cabinet, and by the British ambassador, all of whom were agreed that Naif lacked the necessary qualifications.

I had often heard the opinion expressed among the elite in Amman that Talal's hospitalization was a hoax, a way of ridding the country of an anti-British reformer. I could see why people believed this, because his commitment to his people was clearly evident during his periods of lucidity. Though aware of the uncertainties involved, the cabinet nevertheless determined to place Talal at the helm. They believed that his reign would be short, and that the way would then be open for Hussein, whom they considered Abdullah's most suitable successor. Two physicians were dispatched to Switzerland to evaluate Talal's mental condition. They concluded that Talal had recovered from his illness and was ready to assume leadership, and plans were being made for his return to Amman.

Naif, however, made his own dash for the throne by plotting to arrest the cabinet ministers in office and put in their place a cabinet that would proclaim him monarch. He relied primarily on the loyalty of the Hashemite Regiment, which was in charge of palace security and equipped with armored cars and antitank weapons. The regiment was led by Naif's trusty friend Colonel Habis Majali, the capable officer who was the commander of the Latrun fortress, which blocked the Israelis' advance on Jerusalem in 1948.

Glubb Pasha countered the move by placing two divisions of mechanized infantry on the hills opposite the palace. To avert civil war, Majali withdrew his forces and the coup was aborted. Naif left Jordan. Talal was declared king with much jubilation and fanfare. As the ever optimistic Glubb Pasha put it, "for the moment we hoped that all would once more be well, and that old happy days would come back."

King Talal reigned for less than a year. During his monarchy Jordan's relations with her Arab neighbors and with the Palestinians improved. Talal curbed drug trafficking and, perhaps most important, began moving Jordan's patriarchal autocracy toward a democracy. He established a constitution, giving more power to the parliament and limiting the absolute authority of the king. Together with the able prime minister Abul Huda, Talal governed successfully.

It was becoming increasingly evident, however, that the burdens of office were too great for him to bear. He was buffeted by mood swings, moving from states of rationality to moments of inexplicable rage. Intelligent and efficient when well, he would suddenly turn violent, threatening even members of his own family. A medical report was submitted to the parliament to the effect that the king was suffering from "mental illness, which made it impossible for him to rule and bear responsibility." King Talal abdicated and his son Hussein was named successor.

Hussein, a student at a boarding school in England, was vacationing in Switzerland when a telegram addressed to "His Majesty King Hussein" reached his hotel. He didn't have to read further. A regency council of three was formed to run the affairs of the country until Hussein came of age. Hussein would reach the age of eighteen sooner by the lunar calendar than by the civil calendar, so the lunar calendar was followed. Hussein was crowned within a few months.

I heard the excitement of the crowds during Hussein's coronation, transmitted by shortwave radio, and I saw in the newspapers pictures of Hussein looking confident but so young. I remember seeing him as a boy, first in the backyard of his parents' home, tinkering with his bicycle. It must have been precious to him, that bicycle, for he was often seen either shining it, fixing it, or riding it proudly around the neighborhood. I am glad to see him at the helm now, but I wonder how someone his age, whatever his abilities, can undertake the responsibilities of his office.

I wish I had a crystal ball. Who knows whether King Hussein will be able to hold his own in these difficult times or fall victim to the turbulence of the region? King Farouk has just been deposed and a young colonel named Abdel Nasser has taken over, ending a long-established monarchy in Egypt. A growing republican movement in Iraq is threatening the throne of the Hashemite king Faisal. British power, which supported the rise of the Hashemites after the First World War, is ebbing. The cold war has penetrated the Middle East, militant movements are on the rise — and Abdullah is gone.

I worry for the young king, and I also fear for Israel. How will he approach the neighbor with whom he shares the longest border? Will he follow his grandfather's legacy or will he yield to the radical elements in the Arab world?

I am not the first, nor will I be the last, to ask these questions. Questions like them have been asked by my people since Biblical times. I am reminded of a passage in the Book of Joshua.

> And it came to pass, when Joshua was by Jericho, that he lifted his eye, and looked, and behold, there stood a man over him with his sword drawn in his hand. And Joshua went to him and said unto him: "Art thou with us, or for our adversaries?"

I pray that young King Hussein may lead his people to peace; that he may revive and realize his grandfather's dream.

22

O Jerusalem

Now it is 1967, sixteen years after King Abdullah's assassination, and still I am haunted by its memory. The Six-Day War has just ended in spectacular triumph and Israel is engulfed by a wave of euphoria. The human suffering on both sides was immeasurable, but many hope that it may have been the war to end all wars. Jerusalem is again an integral part of Israel. The cradle of three major religions, the place of the coming of the Messiah, the object of religious longing for Jews, Muslims, and Christians, Jerusalem arouses passions that never wane. The Jewish citizens of the city walk with a renewed confidence in their stride. Children hum "Jerusalem of Gold," a song that has become a second national anthem, a new serenade to an ancient city. It can be heard everywhere, resounding from open windows, balconies, passing vehicles, and outdoor cafes: "Jerusalem of gold, of light, of bronze,/I am the violin for all your songs."

Now that the gates to the Old City are open, I find myself drawn to the place that had been inaccessible to me for two decades. Along with many other Israelis, I keep going back to the courts and alleys I went through on my way to school. I often have to weave through the crowds of Arabs and Israelis engaged in what seems like a recuperation of the past, the reestablishment of old relations. Moving along the main concourse of the soukh, I see men in long black caftans rushing toward the Western Wall. They are the devout, who pour their hearts out in prayer at the most holy of Jewish shrines. Young Israelis in shorts and sandals gather around the stores, examining the merchandise on display, looking for artifacts to add an ethnic touch to their modern apartments. Colorful wool rugs, ornate brass trays and jugs, luminous ceramics are purchased briskly by people engaged in the old and familiar habits of barter.

For me it is neither a desire to pray at the wall nor a search for local color that attracts me to the narrow alleys of the Old City. It is a longing for places that used to be my second home. At the beginning I expected to see the fly-infested open sewers that once flooded the cobblestones, hear the cries of hawkers that used to fill the air, and smell the pungent odors of decaying fruits and the sweet fragrance of freshly baked bread. To my surprise I find a soukh quite cleaner than I remember and the streets in good repair. The open sewers are now covered, the main road neatly paved, and the stores better lit and newly painted. It is only when I turn southward, through the twisted alleys that lead to the Jewish Quarter, that I see the devastation.

The passage to the Western Wall is strewn with trash, the steps and walks leading to it are in ruin, the pavement in front of the Wall is in disrepair, and wild grass grows between the stones. The only familiar sight is the ancient wall and the men crowding in front of it, swaying and praying, touching it with their prayer shawls and bringing their lips to it. Turning around to survey the Jewish Quarter to the west, I see a collapsing arch perilously hanging against the cloudless sky, a remnant of a building of considerable size. I gasp as I recognize it. It was part of the Hurvah Synagogue, though the walls have been pushed down, the dome collapsed, and the main prayer hall strewn with shattered stone and glass. Here I spent the days of my childhood and early adolescence, studying at the yeshiva adjacent to the synagogue. The Hurvah was the first synagogue built in Jerusalem by Ashkenazi Jews in the early part of the eighteenth century. It was destroyed by hostile Muslims shortly after. When a new synagogue was built on top of the ruins, it was therefore named the Hurvah, meaning "ruin." To me it never felt like a ruin, for I saw it in its full glory, shimmering in the bright sun of Jerusalem. I used to admire its magnificent altar and paintings, one depicting a large menorah and the other the tablets of the Ten Commandments. Even when I had given up my religious studies, I continued to visit the synagogue, finding solace and comfort in its cool interior.

I still remember that day of hope and excitement when the Hurvah Synagogue was filled with the devout and the secular who had come to hear Sir Herbert Samuel, the first British high commissioner of Palestine, and a Jew. He had come to join in prayer and to deliver words of reassurance to the Jewish community. "Comfort ye, comfort ye my people!" he read from Isaiah. There was not a dry eye in the synagogue. I also remember the day when the British flag was dedicated at the Hurvah, to celebrate the valor of the Jewish brigade that had fought alongside the British in the

Middle East during the First World War. Like the paintings and the altar, it was gone.

Climbing the broken stone steps toward the center of the Jewish Quarter, I feel sadness and anger welling in me while I remembered the struggle for the Old City in 1948. Back then, the Jewish Quarter consisted of an area of only 36 acres, populated by 1,700 ultra-Orthodox Jews and a garrison of 150 soldiers. They were surrounded by the forces of Abdullah el-Tel, who had placed his batteries on the Mount of Olives and was hurling two hundred shells a day into their midst. Every attempt to break into the Old City and save the beleaguered group had failed. The garrison was reduced to thirty-five men. The inhabitants gathered in the cellars of the three main synagogues, praying for salvation, but as the supply of water, bread, and ammunition was exhausted, they had no choice but to surrender. The Jordanian army shielded the captives from attacks by Arab gangs, released the women, children, and the elderly, and took all able-bodied men captive. This happened on May 28, 1948, a day that marked the end of two thousand years of almost continuous Jewish residence in the Old City.

Jerusalem is again open to us and the Jewish Quarter will soon be rebuilt, but peace has eluded us. After two wars and numerous attempts at negotiations we are still worlds apart. The failure to reach a workable understanding goes back to the early relations between the Hashemites and the Jewish community in Palestine. Soon after he assumed power over Transjordan, Abdullah met with Chaim Weizmann, then president of the World Jewish Organization, to work out an agreement concerning the boundaries between the Jewish and Hashemite states. Abdullah had proposed one of his Semitic Kingdom plans, which was unacceptable to the Jewish community.

In 1937 the British-led Peel Commission recommended the partitioning of Palestine into Jewish and Arab states, the latter comprising 80 percent of the land and to be governed by Abdullah. The proposal was a difficult one for the Jewish community to swallow — and a very toothsome one for Abdullah. Privately rejoicing over the prospect, he even ordered that a golden dagger inscribed "From Abdullah, Sovereign of Both Banks of the Jordan" be sent to the king of England as a token of his appreciation. However, external Arab opposition was so great that the emir was compelled to reject the plan, and the dagger was never delivered.

And so it went. In 1947 Abdullah came very close to accepting the United Nations partition plan for Palestine. He reached an understanding with Golda Meir, whereby Jordan would remain neutral in the event of war and Israel would in turn refrain from interfering with his attempt to annex the Arab part of Palestine. Again Abdullah was unable to withstand the pressure being exerted on him by his Arab neighbors to wage war against the new Jewish state. He joined the war and was given the title of chief commander of the invading Arab forces.

When a temporary cease-fire was reached, Abdullah made a concerted effort to turn it into a lasting peace. He visited other Arab leaders and tried to persuade them to accept the status quo. It is said he told the prime minister of Lebanon that owing to the UN embargo, the Arab Legion had run out of ammunition and there was little to be gained by continuing the fight. "Why don't you shoot oranges at them?" yelled the angry prime minister. "We can't do that," replied Abdullah. "There are no oranges this time of year."

Negotiations continued until Abdullah's death in 1951. At one point, Abdullah was so confident that an agreement had been reached that he handed out flowers to the members of the Israeli and Jordanian negotiating teams. But once again he was unable to finalize the agreement. His own ministers opposed him.

Why is it that we are like two climbers who ascend a mountain and try to meet at the pinnacle, only to retreat without ever reaching the top? I am neither a politician nor an historian, and I know others will find answers more erudite than mine. I am only trying to make some sense of the events as one who lived through them, and because I came to know the man who played such a decisive role in shaping them.

I have witnessed the growth of two antagonistic national movements, Jewish Zionism and Arab nationalism, both competing for the same soil, both asserting their ancestral claim to the land. When my grandparents came to Israel at the end of the nineteenth century, they did not foresee a struggle with the Arabs. Together with other European Jews, they came to build a home for themselves and the Jews dispersed in the Diaspora. And they did not come to a land of lush greenery, abundant in water and rich in resources. It was filled with malaria-infested marshes and forbidding deserts. They planted new orchards, turned the dry deserts into fertile fields, built new cities and revived the old ones. But there was another dream to contend with, the growing national awareness of the Arabs seeking their own identity on the same land. It was a collision of dreams, dreams that hardened into stone walls.

This was something Abdullah seemed to understand. He was not paralyzed by the irrational, visceral animosity felt by so many Arabs toward Jews and Zionism. I was surprised to find him interested in and often openly envious of our achievements, and respectful of our work ethic and our determination. He saw the benefits of undertaking joint projects with the Jews and was willing to consider a variety of ways of dividing the region; we in turn believed that he would help us break out of our isolation.

Perhaps it was a strange kind of hope. His people and mine were so different, our countries based on such divergent values and institutions. His was an absolute monarchy, a nation forged out of warring nomadic tribes, held together by the wisdom and benevolence of a leader and heavily supported by a foreign power; ours was a struggling young democracy united by an ancient creed. He was convinced that he alone knew what was best for his people; we Jews were continually torn apart by internal debate and political strife. He was surrounded by servants, chauffeurs, and luxury, while our leaders lived simply, espousing egalitarian values. When I was visiting the workers' quarter of Tel Aviv, and passed Ben-Gurion's residence, I couldn't help comparing Abdullah's lavish royal court and Ben-Gurion's modest house.

I often think of Sir Alec Kirkbride's story, a story that brings to light the difference between the two leaders. Kirkbride once walked into Abdullah's hotel room in London and saw him shoving banknotes under his pillow.

"What are you doing?" asked Kirkbride.

"I am hiding the money from myself," answered Abdullah.

At the other end of the spectrum is Ben-Gurion, who was so frugal that he used to record even his smallest daily expenses to make sure he didn't exceed his meager budget. One story has it that Ben-Gurion appeared in the Knesset wearing a formal suit and tie, having just returned from a meeting with foreign officials. Addressing the house, he said, "Pardon my appearance. I have not had a chance to get out of my work clothes." How different from Abdullah, with his gold-embroidered Bedouin robes, army uniforms, and expensive Western clothes.

Yet, despite all this, my friendship with Abdullah taught me that the king and the Israeli leaders held one thing in common: a robust sense of the possible and the practical. I remember Abdullah joking about his own pragmatic outlook. "There are times," he would say, "when you have to consider the situation. Imagine you are walking across a bridge and you see a bear coming toward you from the other side. What can you do? You say to the bear, 'Good morning, Auntie, how are you today?'"

Will the young king across the river follow his grandfather's legacy? Will he join us in trying to untangle the mysteries and complexities built into the very essence of our region? Will there come a time when we really mean it when we say *shalom aleichem*, and they *aleikum salaam?*

Part II

From Amman, 1995

23

The Royal Palace Revisited

FOR ME, EL-AL FLIGHT #008, a routine overnight passage from New York to Tel Aviv, was anything but routine. It was the beginning of a journey in my father's footsteps to the royal palace in Amman, made possible by King Hussein's invitation.

As the plane approached Tel Aviv, I saw a whole city shimmering in the light of early morning. The roofs of the buildings glittered with sparks, as if covered by a huge blanket of shiny sequins. This was not some mirage nor the effects of a sleepless night, but rather the reflection of sunlight off the thousands of solar heating panels placed on top of the roofs. A prosaic heating appliance had turned the city into a glorious sight; a magical beginning to a legendary trip.

We stopped at my brother's house in Tel Aviv for an overnight rest. Shortly before four the next morning, the family began to gather. There were fourteen of us, ranging in age from sixteen to seventy-three, all descendants of my parents, Mendel and Tova Cohen — their children, grandchildren, and one great-grandchild. We had converged from different corners of the country to join in a most unusual adventure. Tel Aviv was uncharacteristically quiet that morning, and so were the members of our family as they arrived. We exchanged a few hushed greetings, the usual levity typical of such gatherings much subdued. The bus waiting downstairs reminded us that there was no time for conversation or a cup of coffee. It was essential to get going to avoid the crowds at the crossing.

We rode in silence toward the border, some curling up in half-slumber, some watching the sky lighten. No one seemed disturbed by the constant chatter of the bus radio. There was nothing of importance to listen to until the four o'clock news came on. All was well that morning: no terrorist bombs, no border infiltration, no Katyusha rockets landing on northern villages. We settled back into our comfortable positions, each lost in his or her own thoughts.

The passage across the border filled me with both hope and anxiety. My hope was that in Amman I would find traces of my father's presence and learn more about the meaning of his experiences there. My anxiety was about whether the trip would be safe. I had never felt easy when my father went to Jordan, and now I was feeling the same unease.

It was five o'clock when we arrived at the Sheikh Hussein Terminal, a hurriedly assembled Jordan River crossing point. The sun was already up, drying the mist in the April air as well as the last drops of dew still clinging to the thorn bush. To our great surprise we were not the first to reach the bridge at this early hour. Ahead of us were sixteen buses, some of which had arrived as early as 1:00 A.M. Hundreds of eager tourists were wondering whether they would be among the six hundred permitted to enter Jordan that day. The border office wasn't expected to open until eight, and until then there was no way of knowing who would pass and who would be left behind. Crossing was estimated to occur sometime between ten and three — that is, if we were among the lucky six hundred.

On the eve of our departure I had received a call from the Director of Royal Protocol, offering to arrange for my husband and me to be picked up at the border and driven to Amman. It was a gracious gesture and I had been deeply touched by this expression of hospitality, but I could not see leaving the family behind at the border and heading off in an air-conditioned royal car. I declined the offer as gracefully as I could and made arrangements with the director to meet up in Amman. Waiting around in the heat of the Jordan Valley, however, made me question, if only for a moment, such unconditional family solidarity.

I decided to spend the three hours before the terminal opened trying to ensure that we crossed that day. I learned that the terminal manager on the Israeli side was a man by the name of Yossi, said to be wearing a black T-shirt and smoking a pipe. I found Yossi surrounded by other tourists, all with their own stories and requests for special consideration. Surprisingly, Yossi, a most patient and helpful man, was willing to listen to my story too. I told him that we were guests of King Hussein and that it was essential for us to cross in time to meet his representative, who would be waiting for us in Amman. Yossi's face broke out in a knowing smile. "All of us here are guests of King Hussein," he replied, drawing on his pipe. When I showed Yossi our correspondence with the king and his staff, however, he was duly impressed and made arrangements for our group to be the first to cross into Jordan.

There was plenty of time left to look around. Signs in Hebrew and Arabic, pointing to Jordan in one direction and Israel in the other, replaced the old Do NOT PASS! BEWARE OF MINES! signs. The words BORDER TERMINAL loomed large in both languages. A crowd of Israelis were waiting for the terminal to open, their hopes undaunted by the heat rising in the valley. There was no shade to be found and no place to sit, except for a dozen or so chairs, already occupied, at a single roadside kiosk. I knew Israelis were avid travelers, said to be forever reenacting the legacy of the Wandering Jew, but this willingness to put up with considerable discomfort signified more than the usual tourist enthusiasm.

I understood the magnetic power exerted on Jews by that stretch of land lying east of the Jordan River. Growing up in Israel, I had felt it in my soul, like a yearning for a lost twin. In the past, some political movements in Israel had advocated extending the country to include territory east of the Jordan, but they were on the extreme fringe of the spectrum and no longer active. Still, even average Israelis felt an emotional pull toward a land rich in ancestral connections and ancient memories. This is the land crossed by the Israelites on their way to Canaan, after they had been released from Egypt thousands of years earlier. It contains Mount Nebo, from which Moses had seen the promised land in the west, though he died before he could reach it. It is the land of Moab, home to Ruth the Moabitess, who married a Jew, adopted her husband's religion — and, when he died, remained loyal to her mother-in-law, her new faith, and her new family. Remarried to Boaz from Judea, Ruth was the ancestor of King David.

Jews had populated various parts of Transjordan over

the ages, alternately coming into conflict and living harmoniously with the various tribes in the region. And in the twentieth century, what is now Jordan had been part of the land promised the Jews, later partitioned by the British and given to Abdullah.

Few Israelis traveling along the Jordan can ignore the majesty of the Edom mountains, rising over the plains east of the river. When the sun rises over these mountains it sets the hills ablaze, extending their crimson glow over the endless skies. At noon they take on hues of ocher and red, and at sunset they turn blue, purple, and gold, spreading their gentle glow over the desert below. There, in the red mountains of Edom (which means "red"), lies the ancient city of Petra, meaning "rock." Carved into the cliffs by the Nebateans, Petra's palaces, temples, tombs, theaters, markets, and intricate water systems have been miraculously preserved since the second century B.C.E.

A fad, almost a cult, devoted to a love for the mountains grew up among Israeli youth after the 1948 war. Songs of longing for the red rock and its mysteries were composed, and some of the more adventurous actually attempted to cross the forbidden border and climb up to Petra. A few never returned, presumably discovered by Bedouin and killed.

The less adventurous could gaze at Aqaba's lights from Eilat, or at the farms on the far side of the Jordan Valley, where farmers, almost within earshot, could be seen tilling their land with the same ardor as their Israeli counterparts. So close and yet out of reach. Now that the borders were open, Israelis by the thousands were rushing to satisfy their longing for the land beyond the river.

It took only three minutes to drive from the Israeli side of the terminal to the Jordanian side, but more than two hours for immigration procedures. The customs officers, all men, were lodged in prefabricated sheds, attending to their tasks at a most leisurely pace. There was much back-slapping, handshaking, and salutations with the other Jordanians who came in and out, distracting the officials from their task. The officers took their time to enter by hand the necessary passport data into a large book, and then to copy it slowly onto other forms, apparently enjoying the act of scribing the ornate letters and digits of the Arabic alphabet. Though dressed in dark blue woolen uniforms, they seemed oblivious of the heat. Despite our royal invitation, the time needed to process the documents of the fourteen people in our group felt interminable. Strangely enough, I noticed few Jordanians clamoring at the border to visit Israel — only a trickle of men and women going to visit relatives in the West Bank and Gaza.

Finally we were through, and met by a guide, a police-man, and a driver. All three were to accompany us through-out the trip. The cold bottled water in the air-conditioned minivan was much welcomed, as was the no-nonsense manner with which our guide, Leilah, urged the languid driver to start his motor and get moving.

As we drove through the central part of the Jordan Valley, we could see clusters of unfinished houses with shabby curtains serving as doors and partitions, children running around barefoot, donkeys and mules being used for transportation, and dirty waterholes serving people and animals alike. My father used to talk about Abdullah's frustration with the passivity of his people. Abdullah couldn't help but notice the difference between the green forests, fertile fields, and productive agricultural villages in Israel and the dusty, barren land on this side of the river. The same topography, climate, soil, and accessibility to water existed on both sides of the river, yielding food and plenty on one side, poverty and misery on the other. Whenever he came back from a visit in Palestine, the king would be filled with envy of the lushness of the country, and implore his people to learn from their Jewish neighbors to work harder, to acquire new skills, and to take control of their environment, that they might rise out of poverty. It appeared that little had changed in that region of the country in two generations.

When we reached Amman, however, it was evident that big changes had taken place. We entered the city by way of a wide highway leading to a beautiful broad boulevard lined with public buildings, a modern mosque, a university, city hospitals, museums, and private homes surrounded by vines and fruit trees. As we came closer to the center, we noticed the familiar ills of many large cities — heavy traffic and honking horns. A busy metropolis, Amman is home to half of Jordan's total population.

The hotel, the Grande Forte, was large and bustling. Decorated with bright colors, marble, brass, and colorful carpeting, it bore no resemblance to the intimate and elegant Philadelphia Hotel from days past; rather, it seemed like the sort of luxury hotel you'd find in any other major city. The friendliness and hospitality we had encountered so far were reassuring, though I remembered the Arab custom of extending hospitality to all guests, be they friend or foe. Which were we?

*   *   *

The visit to the royal palace in Amman was to be the highlight of the trip, an event I had planned and waited for with great anticipation. But as with so many great events, trivia intruded. King Hussein's invitation to visit had been extended only to my husband and me. The other members of the family traveling with us were not included. It was becoming evident, however, that they were expecting to be part of the visiting party, though we had agreed earlier to go our separate ways on the day of the palace visit. They kept suggesting that I "do something" to get them invited. My sixteen-year-old niece was open about her feelings. "This is such an emotional experience," she told me with adolescent frankness. "I can't wait to see the palace." My niece added, "Grandpa used to tell me so many stories about the king's court. Now I can see it with my own eyes," and my brother hinted that the family would be very disappointed if a way of getting everyone in was not found. I was reluctant to take advantage of the king's generosity and ask that twelve additional people be included in the visit, but I knew that the other members of my family had as much reason to be there as I did.

When the director of protocol called the next morning to discuss plans for the day, the moment of truth arrived. Feeling uncomfortable about putting him on the spot, I nevertheless, had to ask. "Umm . . ." I began. "You see, our whole family, all the children and grandchildren of Mendel Cohen are on sort of a pilgrimage . . . visiting . . . eager to see what's left of his work. They would very much appreciate an opportunity to join us . . . if possible . . ." I stammered as the director listened patiently.

"How many?" he asked.

"Twelve," I replied, holding my breath.

"Twelve?" Silence. There was a very long pause. "No problem, no problem," he said at last. I breathed a sigh of relief.

We gathered in the lobby of the hotel, our travel sneakers and dungarees replaced by dresses, shoes, and suits. We still couldn't believe we were in Amman. After decades of war we were back, feeling safe, being greeted by the people around us, experiencing first-hand what my father had experienced decades earlier.

Two vehicles were waiting at the entrance to the hotel: a chauffeur-driven royal car and a van, which we used throughout the trip. Being the senior members of the group, my husband and I were assigned to the royal car, while the rest of the family, accompanied by a guide and an armed policeman, followed in the van.

The city looked nothing like the pastoral village of my memories. Wide roads, traffic lights, impatient drivers, and gasoline fumes had replaced camels and donkeys. Cars honked where vendors used to hawk their goods, and the brownish-red roads of old Amman were paved over. Approaching the palace compound, our vehicles proceeded through several miles of lush gardens, fountains, and tree-shaded winding boulevards to the first entry gate. The large ornamented gate, covered with gold leaf, was heavily guarded. We were stopped by the palace security. To our great surprise, our Jordanian police escort was asked to step out of the car and remain outside the gate. Our party was then signaled ahead. We learned later that Ahmed, our escort, was not trusted because he did not belong to the elite guard assigned to protect the king.

We were driven to a second, equally impressive gilded gate, where we were met by Brigadier Amari, chief of security. Brigadier Amari, an energetic man in his forties, was dressed in a crisp khaki army uniform decorated with medals. Particularly impressive was his beret, which was spangled with golden stars. He greeted us in perfect English, ready to guide the group through the palace and eager to ensure the success of the visit. He escorted us to the third gate, the final security point. Getting through this gate required the presence of the chief of security himself.

It was at that point that I became aware of the unusual privilege accorded us by our hosts. Here we were — now fifteen, the family plus our tour guide, instead of two — being permitted entry into one of the most heavily guarded places in the country at very short notice. Hospitality had outweighed security considerations, a gesture of goodwill undoubtedly endorsed by King Hussein. And this is how we found ourselves in front of Raghdan Palace.

We stood there in silence. The building had hardly changed in fifty years. The white facade built of cut limestone, the arched sentry posts, the latticed front window, and the balconies of the wings once used as the women's residences — these were the same. The old Turkish cannons still faced Amman.

There were changes, of course. The road leading to the entrance, once a direct path, now curved around the building, making access possible only through the side — probably a security measure. A series of concrete fortifications, camouflaged by terraced flower gardens, had been placed at the entrance to the palace. We pulled out our cameras to get a shot of the facade and were promptly asked to refrain from taking any photographs. The palace was neither a tourist attraction nor a residence for the king and his family. It was, rather, a closely guarded citadel used for special occasions and accessible only to a few.

Brigadier Amari explained that the interior had been entirely renovated in 1992 and that none of the elements built by my father were likely to have remained. Nonetheless, the palace felt familiar to me. In the entrance hall, an inlaid marble design of a star, or the sun, had replaced the water fountain that had once stood there. On either side of the entrance were wide marble steps leading to the second level. I thought of my father's story about those stairs. They had originally been made of white marble, but Abdullah had found them slippery, uneven, and hard on his feet. My father replaced them with wooden steps, giving them a homier feel. Now they were marble again, transformed to follow the changing cycles of taste and style.

A parlor to the left of the entrance attracted my attention, for it was a room my father had often mentioned and on which he had done quite a bit of work. I recognized the ornate ceiling he had described. Having recently been restored, it was in glorious full color, its intricate designs framed by gold leaf, reflecting the Ottoman artistic heritage. Cabinets along the walls displayed a variety of gifts received by King Hussein. They had replaced the cabinets built by my father for Abdullah's trophies.

We mounted the stairs and entered the Great Hall. My eyes focused on the floor. It was, after all, what had brought my father to Amman in the first place. And here it was, in its full beauty. Although not the original floor installed by my father, it retained his design. Stained glass windows let in a soft light, giving the floor a sheen. A new ceiling made of intricately carved wood complemented the floor and gave the room a feeling of openness and elegance. On a platform stood the throne. I was struck by its simplicity. It was really no more than a comfortable chair of unassuming proportions. I remembered my father's story regarding Abdullah's ambivalence about his succession, and consequently about the type of throne he had wanted built. Modest though it was, there was nothing temporary-looking about this throne, nor about any other aspect of the palace.

I found it difficult to pull myself away from the Great Hall. Renovated or not, it retained my father's signature.

Roaming through the rooms and halls, I discovered that the original layout of the building had remained unchanged. The doors leading to the old harem were still there. Today its rooms are used for administrative purposes. The room adjacent to the Great Hall, formerly a dining room, was now used as a conference room and furnished with long tables and chairs. A loft in the dining room had once served as a platform for after-dinner entertainment but had been removed, leaving the room looking rather bare.

Two other rooms on the second floor caught my attention. One was locked and had a plaque on its door, indicating that it was here that Hussein ibn Ali, King Abdullah's father, had died. Next to it was a room that had served as Abdullah's private office. The room was dark and musty, its old mauve curtains drawn shut. A large desk sat in the middle of the room but its surface was bare. It was a sad-looking place, barren and neglected. As we were about to leave, finding nothing of particular interest in it, my niece exclaimed, "Look at that!" Pointing to the ceiling chandelier, she said,

"It's the exact same fixture grandma used to have in her house." It was indeed identical to a fixture that used to hang in my parents' home in Jerusalem. When he purchased the fixture for King Abdullah's office, my father must have bought two, hanging one in Abdullah's palace and one in his own house in Jerusalem. The chandelier in Jerusalem is long gone, lost when the house was sold, but its twin in Amman had survived.

Walking through the palace, touching walls, opening and shutting doors, peering into rooms and passageways, I could feel my father's presence. Ironically, it seemed more difficult to find traces of Abdullah. I had expected to see King Abdullah's pictures displayed everywhere, to find his trophies, his letters, his personal copy of the Koran. To my surprise, none were to be found. Hoping to look through some original documents and photos, I asked permission to visit the library my father had built. I was told that the library was no longer in existence. A few pictures were stored in the basement of the palace, we were told, but the cellar was inaccessible. Pictures of King Hussein were proudly displayed, as was appropriate, but where, I wondered, was Abdullah?

"And Abdullah's grave? Could we visit and pay our respects?" we asked. "There is nothing special to see," we were told. It was a simple grave of no particular distinction, located somewhere on the palace grounds. I thought of Abdullah's funeral and burial, which had been conducted quietly to prevent violence from escalating. I suspected that the memory of the founder of the country was still being kept muted so as not to inflame the same passions that had brought about his death.

Still, we had found more than we had hoped merely by coming to the palace. We had found that the legacy of peace was being carried on by Abdullah's grandson, and by the children and grandchildren of Mendel Cohen. It was reaffirmed by the fact of our presence at the very heart of the Hashemite Kingdom, where an Arab king and an Israeli carpenter had once worked together.

24

Amman, Beyond
the Palace Gates

ONLY UPON LEAVING THE PALACE GROUNDS did I become aware of the distance between the palace and the streets of Amman. Surrounded by a large security force, protected by fortifications, and locked behind gilded gates, the palace and its compound seemed insulated and inaccessible. In its silent majesty, the palace was a stark contrast to the some of the dilapidated buildings in the surrounding areas, and the noise of the bustling streets.

Our guide had never even been inside Raghdan Palace and asked if she could accompany us into the inner sanctum. This she did against her father's advice. The night before, he had cautioned her about going in. "The walls have ears and you can never be sure," he'd told her. Ears to listen to what? I wondered. She never told us, but on our way out, having expressed her appreciation for this unique opportunity, she asked us if we would write a letter on her behalf, explaining the circumstances of her presence in the palace. She was worried about the implications of her visit.

My first visit to Amman had occurred when I accompanied my father on a rare and exciting trip, but I had already learned about this ancient city as an elementary school student. I had looked up a chapter in Genesis, strangely skipped by my Bible teacher. I read it and discovered why. The chapter told a story of forbidden deeds considered unfit for young children:

When the cities of Sodom and Gomorra were destroyed, only three people were saved — Lot, nephew of Abraham, and his two daughters. They survived because Abraham pleaded before God to spare Lot who was the only just man in the cities of sin. Lot and his daughters went to dwell in a cave.

> The older one said to the younger one, "Our father is old, and there is no man on earth to consort with us in the way of all the world. Come, let us make our father drink wine, and let us lie with him, that we may maintain life through our father." That night they made their father drink wine, and the older one went and lay with her father; he did not know when she lay down and when she rose.

> The next day the older one said to the younger, "See, I lay with our father last night. Let us make him drink wine tonight also, and you go and you lie with him, that we may maintain life through our father." That night they also made their father drink wine, and the younger one went and lay with him; he did not know when she lay down or when she rose. Thus the two daughters of Lot came to be with child by their father. The older one bore a son and called him Moab; he is the father of the Moabites today. And the younger

also bore a son; and she called him Ben-Ammi [son of my parental kindred]; he is father of the Ammonites today.

The Ammonites built themselves a city called Ammon, later to be called Rabbat-Ammon, thought to go back to the second millennium B.C.E. and settled by tribes that had migrated southward from Mesopotamia. Amman was invaded repeatedly over the centuries — by the Israelites, Assyrians, Persians, and the Greeks who followed in the footsteps of Alexander the Great and named the city Philadelphia, City of Brotherly Love, after the incestuous love between King Ptolemy II and his sister. They made it part of their Decapolis, a loosely affiliated group of ten cities holding a monopoly on trade along the route from the Middle East to the Orient. The Romans invaded the region after the Greeks. The glorious Greek, Roman, and Byzantine temples, theaters, and arcades, as well as the flourishing economy they had brought to the region, deteriorated with the desertification of the area by the incursion of nomad Arab tribes and grazing herds.

It was also through Bible study that I learned of the fragile peace between the Israelites and their Ammonite neighbors. When the Israelites were delivered from Egypt and crossed the desert on their way to Canaan, they passed through the land now called Transjordan. They were instructed by Moses to refrain from doing battle with the Ammonites because of the common lineage between Abraham and his nephew Lot, the presumed progenitor of the Ammonites.

You are now passing through the territory of Moab through Ar. You will then be close to the Ammonites. Do not harass them or start a fight with them for I will not give any part of the land of the Ammonites to you as a possession. I have given it as a possession to the descendants of Lot.

Despite this admonition, territorial disputes between the Israelites and their Ammonite neighbors persisted. Strife followed amity, antagonism melted into friendship. King Saul defeated the Ammonites in battle by occupying the Amman Seil, the main source of water for the people of Ammon. He did not conquer their land but subjugated the Ammonites and ended their incursions into the land of Israel. King David defeated the Ammonites and conquered and sacked Rabbat-Ammon. It was then that David committed a most serious transgression. One day, as he was strolling on the roof of his house, he saw a beautiful woman bathing. She was Bat-Sheba, wife of Uriah, a loyal and capable soldier. The king coveted Uriah's wife and sent for her. She came to him and she conceived. David sent Uriah to take part in a fierce battle with the Ammonites and the young man was killed. David then married Bat-Sheba, who gave birth to Solomon, David's successor to the throne. When Solomon became king he made peace with the Ammonites and married one, who gave birth to a son named Rehavam ("the people will prosper"), to signify what he anticipated as the result of this union.

But the Amman of my imagination was made up not just of stories from the Old Testament but from my father as well. In my mind's eye I saw a distant, mysterious city, inhabited by men in long gowns and women in long black dresses and veils. I remember imagining the city's bazaar as a maze of interconnected dark and narrow alleys, where cats, dogs, and sheep roamed at night in search of bits of food. It would wake to the calls of vendors carrying baskets filled with fruits and vegetables and trays of cheese, bread, and honey-soaked cakes on their heads. The Amman that I saw as an adolescent fifty years ago was neither mysterious nor majestic. It resembled some of the larger Arab villages around Jerusalem. The sound of the language, the clothes, the hearty manner of greeting and parting, the chaotic market, the noise and the dust — I remember how cozy and familiar they had all felt.

Later in my youth, Amman was the enemy city, the headquarters of the Arab Legion that had taken Jerusalem's Old City and shelled my parents' home.

The history of the relations between Israel and Jordan is characterized by strange contradictions, twists and turns, states of war and moments of peace. Yet peace was never, at any point, totally dead. There had been de facto cooperation between the countries even during the worst periods of conflict. The bridges across the Jordan were kept open, for example, facilitating the movement of agricultural goods from Jordan to Israel and carrying Israeli products to markets in Arab countries — even when war had been declared between the two countries. There were times when Israel had actually intervened to assist Jordan during periods of crisis, such as in 1958, when a coup took place in Iraq and King Faisal, Hussein's cousin, was killed by a mob on the streets of Baghdad. Hussein had refused to recognize the new regime, and Iraq cut off oil supplies. Saudi Arabia, the

Hashemites' old enemy, tightened the noose around Jordan by withholding oil shipments too. Lacking energy resources and facing the real danger of total shutdown, Hussein appealed to the U.S. for help. The American government, however, was unable to deliver the oil, because the Arab countries surrounding Jordan prohibited the passage of American planes over their airspace. Israel was the only country that permitted American cargo planes to pass over its territory and deliver the oil to Jordan.

And in 1970, when a state of war still existed between the two countries, Jordanian Palestinians under the leadership of Yasir Arafat attempted to topple the monarchy. "Jordan is ours. Palestine is ours, and we shall build our national unity on the whole of the land after having freed it from the Zionist presence, and the reactionary-traitor Hussein presence," declared Arafat. Hussein unleashed the Arab Legion, which chased the PLO out of Jordan. To assist the PLO, and to gain its own foothold in Jordan, Syria sent its tanks rolling toward Amman. Hussein called President Nixon for help, and Nixon called Yitzhak Rabin, then Israel's ambassador to Washington. Within a few hours, in broad daylight, Israeli tanks were heading for the Syrian border. Syria withdrew its tanks from Jordanian soil.

Stories are now surfacing about clandestine negotiations between Israel and Jordan over the last two decades. One such story, relayed by British intelligence, involves mysterious events at a medical center in London. Whenever King Hussein went to England for his routine checkups, Israeli government leaders also scheduled their medical visits at the same center and at the same time. It is no longer a secret that King Hussein has held more secret meetings with Israeli politicians than any other Arab leader.

Mindful of this strange history, we set out to learn more about present-day Amman. Through the offices of King Hussein, arrangements were made for my husband and me to meet Professor Mohammad Bakhit, president of Al al-Bayt University and an expert on Abdullah and his times. Bakhit is currently overseeing the publication of King Abdullah's collected papers.

We were picked up by one of the royal chauffeurs, a short stocky man in his late thirties sporting a heavy, well-trimmed black mustache and well-pressed military uniform. His command of English was limited, but with the little Arabic I remembered from my high school years, we managed a rudimentary conversation. His name, he told us, was Ali Majali. Majali? The name rang a bell. Was our driver related to Habis Majali, the Jordanian war hero and head of security for the late King Abdullah? No, he replied, laughing. He explained that there were many Majalis in Jordan, all descendants of the Majali tribe in the south, now living in urban areas and occupying various government positions. I knew of the Majali tribe, of their rebellion against Abdullah during the early years of his reign and their unwavering support of the monarchy ever since.

Following a brief chat and the customary cup of black coffee, Professor Bakhit presented us with the first four volumes of King Abdullah's writings. The cover of one of the volumes bore a color photograph of the king, looking confident in his white silk kaffiyeh and golden headband. Another depicted the ornate ceiling of Raghdan Palace. A golden crown, symbol of the Hashemite monarchy, appeared at the top of each cover.

"These volumes contain a wide range of Abdullah's writings — speeches and letters he used to write in his own hand and which were published in numerous magazines, often under a pen name. He was also a prolific poet," Professor Bakhit told us. "Some of his poems have been published and are now being collected, but some had never been committed to paper. They were often created spontaneously and delivered orally on the spot."

I shared with President Bakhit a story my father had told about King Abdullah the poet.

"Two Bedouins," I began, "appeared at King Abdullah's palace one day to plead on behalf of their brother. The brother had killed one of his tribesmen and was awaiting final sentencing. The king appeared to ignore their appeal. Instead, he invited them to have lunch with him. At the table Abdullah spoke about topics seemingly unrelated to the Bedouins' petition. He quoted phrases from the Koran, then began to improvise an obscure poem. The first stanza described a man chained to the wall in a prison cell, the second described the suffering of a prisoner's family, and the last ended with words of praise for the *sulkha*, the Bedouin peace ceremony. The king then asked his scribe to read the poem aloud. The scribe did so, raising his voice on the last stanza. Mohammed Zubati, the court manager, who was a master at interpreting the king's intentions, understood what the poem meant and immediately called the prison warden, informing him that Sayidna had pardoned the prisoner and wished him to be set free."

Professor Bakhit nodded his head with evident pleasure. "So — a poet delivering a royal decree!" he exclaimed.
Stories and niceties exchanged, we began a more focused discussion.

"How is the late King Abdullah regarded by the citizens of Jordan today?" we asked.

"Abdullah was a politician of great vision," he responded. "He was misunderstood by many in his generation, but recently there has been a resurgence of interest in
his life and a growing respect for his accomplishments. People
are now realizing that the late king planted the seeds of
peace, and I believe that most of the people today want
peace."

"Why is it, then, that we see so little of King Abdullah's
presence at Raghdan Palace and in Amman — no pictures,
no monuments commemorating his achievements?" we inquired.

"Well, we do have places named after him and there is
a growing recognition of his achievements. Just the fact that
we are working to collect his writings stands as a tribute to
his contributions. But there was a period when his image
was played down, because his policies were not appreciated
and his peace policy criticized. All this is changing now." He
looked with pride at the bound volumes of Abdullah's collected papers.

"Do you believe that King Hussein will be able to over-
come the obstacles to peace which his grandfather was unable to conquer?"

"Yes, I do," he replied. "The time is right. With the end
of the cold war, more moderate forces are emerging in the

Arab world. Our leaders recognize — and hopefully the people too — that the only way to create a better standard of living and a more stable society is through peace in the Middle East. Isn't that also what your leaders believe? We hope that an improved economy and expanded educational opportunities will help our people make progress."

"And what about the emerging power of militant Muslim fundamentalism and political extremism in the Arab world and in Jordan? To what extent do they present a serious threat to King Hussein and his peace policies?"

"The king and his brother the crown prince are very popular with the majority of the people in Jordan," he said reassuringly. "There is an opposition, of course, and it can be quite loud, but hopefully, with a peace settlement in the rest of the Middle East, the voice of the fanatics will weaken."

We asked about the succession to the throne, and why Crown Prince Hassan, Hussein's brother, rather than one of the king's sons, was named successor. He explained that Prince Hassan is a most capable man, a graduate of Oxford fluent in several languages, who carries the vision of a regional economic cooperation with Israel and is responsible for the planning and implementation of joint projects with Israel.

Returning to the topic of Abdullah, Professor Bakhit spoke about the former king's less-known accomplishments, such as the creation of vocational schools for boys, and pioneering the education of women. It is not surprising, added our host, that Jordan now has the largest number of college graduates in the Arab world, with four institutions of higher learning in Amman.

We asked President Bakhit to tell us about the Al al-Bayt University. He told us that the name al-Bayt literally means "the home," but that metaphorically it refers to the prophet Mohammed. The university promotes Islamic studies and a strong Islamic identity, while concurrently offering courses on other cultures and religions. King Abdullah himself was able to integrate these two elements in his own life. He was a devout Muslim whose origins went back to Mecca and who began and ended his day by reading the Koran. But he was also exposed to the cosmopolitan city of Istanbul at an impressionable age and absorbed its ways and tastes. It was this breadth and diversity of experience that laid the foundation for his open-mindedness, his attempt to create a bridge between the Arab world and the West, and the creation of Al al-Bayt university.

Professor Bakhit's response to my next question was to me the most poignant of his comments.

"What in your opinion was Abdullah's greatest and most unique personal asset?" I asked him.

He did not have to think long before speaking. "He knew how to separate the personal from the political. He made friends with people he did not fully agree with politically, and was admired by many who were his political opponents."

These words distilled what I had always seen as the essence of the unique relationship between my father and the king. Both were blessed with the capacity to grow beyond religious, national, and cultural roots, and to relate to each other with respect, trust, and appreciation. They could do this, not because their personal beliefs were superficial and their emotional commitments hollow, but on the contrary because they were both strongly anchored in their heritages. Good bridges need strong supports.

On the way back from Professor Bakhit's office, the chauffeur offered to take us on a tour of Amman the following morning. When he came to pick us up at the hotel, I saw him engaged in a friendly conversation with other drivers. Judging by the laughter and frequent backslapping, the drivers seemed like a most congenial bunch, reminding me of my father's stories about this group closely knit by their love of vehicles and grapevine gossip.

I asked the driver to take us to the downtown area to see the old Philadelphia Hotel, the Diwan — the old government house — and the archeological site of the old Roman theater. He smiled apologetically. The hotel and the old Diwan were gone, he explained, torn down to make room for a new Diwan, a shopping mall, and a parking lot. He offered to take us there.

On the way downtown we drove through several sections of the city. Amman is a city built on seven hills some 2500 feet above sea level, home to 1.5 million inhabitants. It has seen rapid growth in the last three decades, mostly due to immigration from Palestine, Lebanon, and the Gulf Emirates. We were struck by the unusual cleanliness of the streets. There was no graffiti, nor any sign of vandalism.

Like other large urban centers, Amman too has its neighborhoods, dividing the rich, the super-rich, the despondently poor, and the strata in between. Closer to the heart of the city, near the old market, is the older quarter, populated primarily by Palestinians, once refugees and now citizens. The yellowish brown peeling facades of their apartment houses, which are built nearly on top of each other, tell of neglect and squalor. Few women were in sight, but the men were out on the streets in substantial numbers, their idleness reflective of Jordan's high unemployment, which is particularly severe in this area. At the other extreme, farther up in the hills, lie the attractive villas of the rich. Built of cut stone, they are surrounded by well-kept shrubs, flower beds, and vine-covered pergolas. Many of these homes are owned by Palestinian businessmen and professionals who have both contributed to and taken advantage of the growing economy.

The downtown was totally unrecognizable to me. New mosques had been erected there, one incorporating into its structure the original thirteenth-century mosque and large enough to accommodate two thousand worshippers. Shops around the area were selling Western goods, such as clothes and plastic toys and utensils, as well as Bedouin crafts.

Dominating the downtown is the Roman theater, dating back to the beginning of the Christian era. The theater was the only part of the downtown that looked familiar. Hugging the side of the hill, it is now surrounded by scores of bleak-looking houses. With its curved lines and columns of carved white stone, the theater sparkled under the bright sky like a translucent crescent amid drab mediocrity.

Looking around, I sensed something was missing. At first I couldn't put my finger on it. Then I realized what it was — the stream that had once run through town, a stream so clear you could see your reflection over the pebbles at the bottom. Where was it? The driver explained rather proudly that the stream had been diverted into an underground tunnel and was a major source of water for the city. At times it got contaminated by sewer seepage, he added apologetically.

Memories came back to me of the stream and its bed, the wadi. Winding its way among fragrant oleander, fig, olive, and box trees, the wadi was once a place where families gathered in late afternoon when the air began to cool. *Minsham el hawwah* they used to call the practice — a stroll to take in a breath of fresh air. The men would walk ahead of the women, the older among them with their arms behind their backs, worry beads in their hands. Young fathers would carry their children on their shoulders, while the women would tag along behind or sit together on the rocks to exchange gossip and advice. I ached for the loss of the idyllic spot. I found it difficult to accept the reality that the bucolic Jordan of my early memories had been swept away by the course of time, which turns quiet villages into noisy cities, pristine streams into polluted underground rivers, and pastoral fields into paved roads.

I asked our guide to take us to the bazaar. There, at least, I hoped to see more of the old Amman. This time I was not disappointed. It was true that the vendors sold their spices and legumes in plastic bags instead of the newspaper cones of the past, but they were no less charming than before. The minute a customer enters a store, a cup of black coffee instantly appears, and the time-honored process of negotiating begins. Let the novice beware! I went into one of the stores to buy a brass coffeepot. The merchant quoted his price and I offered a lower price. We went through a series of accommodations, he lowering his price and I slowly raising mine. When we finally settled and I walked out with my shiny pot, I discovered that I had ended up paying a higher price than the merchant originally quoted.

We sat down for a snack of almond cakes and cardamom-flavored coffee at one of the small cafés and watched the passersby, a colorful variety of men and women, some carrying their goods on their backs, others riding donkeys or bicycles, all yelling to make way as they passed with large trays on their heads. There were men sitting at the door of another café, smoking a nargileh and manipulating their worry beads. Music blasted from a radio and the chanting of the muezzin could be heard calling the faithful to prayer.

That evening, back in the lobby of the hotel, we came across an English-language paper that discussed Crown Prince Hassan's report on the progress of the peace process. Hassan assured the people that economic cooperation and peace with Israel would bring a higher standard of living and reduce unemployment. A number of joint projects were mentioned — the exploitation of the chemicals in the Dead Sea (an endeavor first initiated by King Abdullah and Israeli concerns), the sharing of precious water resources, the construction of an international airport, and a winter spa along the shores of the Red Sea between Eilat and Aqaba. No longer separated by mines and barbed wire, these two cities would be connected by a promenade, attracting Europeans in search of winter sun. Entrepreneurs would build hotels in the no-man's land. And on the gulf sailboats would cruise where gunboats used to patrol. The article ended with the words, "If Singapore could do it, why can't we?"

Next to us in the lobby were two Jordanian businessmen. They knew a few Hebrew phrases, which they were eager to practice. We found them delightful company and spent the evening chatting. We discovered that they were brothers, partners in a knitwear factory in Amman, and that they had recently visited Israel to explore the possibility of developing a joint manufacturing project. The deal was never finalized. "You have to understand," they explained, "we could have developed a good product together, but we weren't sure that in the end we wouldn't be swallowed up. The Israelis are so knowledgeable and skillful. They could easily have taken over."

The next morning we were preparing for a trip to Petra and met a group of Israeli tourists gathered in the hotel lobby. One of them had a bad toothache and had just returned from a visit to a dentist. The dentist had refused to treat him because of pressure from his professional association to deny service to "tourists," a euphemism for Israelis. I would have ignored this episode had not a similar incident been reported in the *New York Times* around the same time. A Jordanian lawyer known for his pro-peace activities had been disbarred by the Jordanian Bar Association for his frequent and visible contacts with Israeli colleagues and clients.

A chilling incident occurred when we stopped at a shady roadside restaurant for a cold drink. I saw what looked like a newspaper left behind on the table next to us and picked it up. It was a poorly duplicated printed broadsheet with three blurred photographs on it: of King Abdullah, King Hussein, and the late Egyptian president Anwar Sadat. The caption under the pictures read "The Killer Missed One."

The next day brought better news. In the village of

Azraq, an oasis situated close to the Iraqi border, we came across a mother and four barefooted children baking bread on an outdoor *taboon*, a dome-shape wood-burning oven. The woman stopped her work and offered us a taste of her hot flatbread. It was delicious. We asked if we could buy more of it. The woman took all the flat loaves she had baked that afternoon and packed them in a large plastic bag, which she handed over to us. She refused to accept the money we offered and continued to push the bread at us as her children jumped and yelled, "Shalom! Shalom!"

Our visit to Jordan, so limited in time and scope, had brought a mixture of warm expressions of friendship and cold shoulders — endorsements of the peace agreement between Israel and Jordan and reactions of caution and even hostility.

I was remembering the signing of the peace treaty between Jordan and Israel in the Aravah Desert in 1994. The night before, winds swept across the desert, blowing sand in streams and swirls, cutting through everything in their path. The stage set up for the ceremony toppled over, visitors' chairs were strewn everywhere, and the whole area was covered by a heavy blanket of sand. It was as if the elements were conspiring. But the wind subsided before dawn, the stage was rebuilt, the chairs brushed off and put back in place: everything was ready for the five thousand visitors who came from around the world to witness the momentous event.

The Aravah Wadi is a strip of desert lying between Jordan and Israel south of the Dead Sea. For decades it had been surrounded by minefields. Though most of the mines had been removed in preparation for the peace ceremony, guests were cautioned not to wander from the cordoned area.

Children of Jordanian war victims offered flowers to Yitzhak Rabin, former commander in chief of the Israeli armed forces, and children of Israeli victims gave flowers to King Hussein, the commander of a once hostile army.

From the podium King Hussein spoke in a voice choked with emotion. "This is peace with dignity. This is peace with commitment. This is a gift to our people and the generations to come. It will herald the change in the quality of life for people. It will be real."

Prime Minister Rabin spoke next. "We must both draw on the springs of our great spiritual resources to forgive the anguish we caused to each other, to clear the minefield that divided us for many years and to supplant it with fields of plenty."

The treaty was signed on an island of peace surrounded by minefields.

25

Shalom and *Salaam* Are the Same Word

LEILAH WAS THE FIRST PERSON TO GREET US on Jordanian soil and the last to bid us farewell. The Office of Tourism had assigned her to be our guide and to oversee our itinerary and accommodations in Jordan. She was a handsome woman in her mid-forties, and wore dark blue cotton slacks, a leather belt that could have come straight from SoHo, New York, and a pair of sturdy walking shoes. Her sun-bleached hair was neatly tied in the back, making her look like an American suburbanite doing her daily errands rather than like the Arab women of my early memories. She spoke excellent English, though with a slight accent, sometimes substituting *b* for *p*, a sound that does not exist in Arabic. Articulate and knowledgeable, she exuded confidence and energy. It was a new world, I thought, ready to embrace a liberated Arab woman breaking through the old code of male dominance.

I soon discovered, however, that my early enthusiasm about the new Arab woman had been premature. Leilah had difficulty holding her own even with the driver and the policeman who accompanied us, though they were working for her. As soon as we boarded the minivan at the border, Leilah and the two men got into an argument. We had asked whether our itinerary could be altered, so that we could visit the old cities Um Qais and Jerash on our way to Amman. This meant taking a longer route and reaching Amman a few hours later than had been planned. Leilah was willing but, though my Arabic was limited, I understood that her two male assistants were reluctant to make the change. Leilah's reminding them that she was in charge of the itinerary made no difference. The driver continued to raise objections until a call to the central office instructed him to follow Leilah's orders. Time was lost, the temperature in the van was rising, and Leilah was visibly aggravated. This was the first of several episodes in which the driver, sometimes in collusion with the policeman, balked at Leilah's instructions. Later, when I felt freer to ask more sensitive questions, I asked Leilah why the men were so recalcitrant. She explained that Jordanians had difficulty shedding generations of male supremacy. "It's like the war between the sexes in your country," she said with a smile.

I watched the women of Amman from the window of our van and saw they were dressed in a variety of styles. Some wore dresses and skirts, high heels, and makeup, though the hem of the dress never rose above the knee. Miniskirts were nowhere to be seen. I noticed, however, that quite a few of the younger women seemed to prefer traditional Arab garb — those long-sleeved shapeless dresses reaching below their ankles, scarves covering their heads and foreheads.

"The young usually break from tradition and challenge conventional dress codes," I noted to Leilah. "It seems to be different here."

"That may be true of other places," she replied, "but

here many young people are moving back toward traditional ways."

"Is this true of more than just clothes?" I asked.

"Not so much among the Christians, but it seems this way among the Muslims," she replied.

I wanted to ask whether it was an expression of a growing fundamentalism in Jordan, but I didn't. It would take more time and greater familiarity to raise this rather sensitive topic.

I also noticed that large numbers of apartment buildings were being built throughout the city. Made of chiseled stone, these newer buildings were rather attractive, but there was something unusual about them. I realized that many had no balconies, and that their windows were disproportionately small and narrow. From a distance they looked like white fortresses. Leilah picked up on my quizzical look and offered an explanation.

"You probably noticed the small number of balconies. Our people value privacy. They would rather look out than have others look in."

I couldn't help wondering whether this wasn't merely a justification for isolating women from the outside, and whether the old harem mentality described in my father's journal still existed. On the one hand, great progress toward recognizing women's rights had clearly been made. Polygamy was no longer practiced, and Jordanian women were able to attain an education both at home and abroad. On the other hand, watching Leilah and her difficulties with the driver and the policeman told me that the tradition of male supremacy was deeply embedded.

Despite our differences in age, religion, and cultural

background, Leilah and I discovered that we had much in common, that our lives paralleled each other's in uncanny ways. Orthodox Armenian, Leilah was part of a very small minority in Jordan. She had been born in Amman, however, and considered herself Arab first and Christian second. Her grandparents had emigrated from Turkey to Syria at the time of the Armenian massacre in Ottoman Turkey. A son and grandson of millers, Leilah's father built a flour mill in Damascus. When he married a Greek Orthodox woman, he decided to move to Jerusalem, home to larger communities of Armenians and Greek Orthodox, hoping to find greater religious freedom. He built a second flour mill, on the southern outskirts of the city in the town of Beit-Tsafafa. His mill was destroyed by Israeli commandos during the war of 1948. The family moved again, this time to Amman, where Leilah's father built a new flour mill. There he awaited the birth of his first son. He was deeply disappointed when his wife gave birth to a daughter, followed by three more. He thus earned one of the most pejorative titles an Arab man can bear — *Abu Bannat*, or "father of daughters." Nevertheless, with the help of his sons-in-law he established a successful food-processing business in Jordan.

The story of Leilah's family struck a powerful chord in me. My maternal grandfather Sholem had also been a miller, and was the son and brother of millers. Sholem was born in Jerusalem's Old City and practiced his trade there until he married my grandmother Rebecca. They moved into a new neighborhood located outside the walls. He got a job as a miller in a new mill located in the valley east of the walled city, one of the first mechanized mills in the region. The mill was small enough to be run by one man, and my grandfather ran it with great efficiency. He was a quiet man, devoted to his family, his synagogue, and his work. He worked from sunrise to sunset, never taking a day off except for the Sabbath and holidays. Every day at noon, my grandmother would walk down the hill to bring him his meal. He would eat it quickly and then go back to work.

The only time my grandfather took time off was when my friends and I stopped by to see him at the mill. He would stop the machines, take a long rope, tie the ends to the rafters, then attach some flour sacks. The swing would send us flying high, from rafter to rafter. And when it was time to get off, we jumped rapturously into piles of grain. I didn't always visit my grandfather just to use the swing. The mill and my grandfather's work intrigued me. Belts, gears, and bolts turned the grindstone in a slow heartbeat rhythm, grinding the wheat and moving it into a large oscillating sieve, and finally filling sack after sack with fine white flour, spreading a fragrant dust that entered my nostrils and clung to my hair and eyelashes.

The mill was destroyed in 1948 — just like Leilah's father's mill — by Jordanian forces. My grandparents' house was also hit and they moved in with us. My grandfather aged rapidly, almost fading away. Unlike Leilah's father, he was too old to start all over again. He used to take walks, his hands behind his back, read the newspapers, and say little. His hearing was failing and so was his health. He died two years later.

After I had told Leilah the story of my grandfather's mill, she went back to her father to find out more about his mill. It turned out that her father and my grandfather used to sell their flour to the largest bakery in Jerusalem. Leilah and I began to feel connected; it was as if we had known each other in the past, as partners rather than enemies.

A more direct and honest exchange opened up between us. I learned that Leilah was divorced and that after the divorce she had moved in with her parents. She had then briefly moved into an apartment of her own, but found that even her closest female friends stopped visiting her. A woman living by herself was looked upon with suspicion, and anyone befriending her was equally suspect. To break out of her isolation she had had to return to live under her parents' roof and thumb, as all single women do.

I admired Leilah's resilience and courage. I often wondered what opportunities she had missed and what her life would have been had she lived in a more open society. Vibrant, intelligent, and adaptive, she could have achieved so much. Nonetheless, unbowed, she had built a life of her own and, most important, had not forgotten how to laugh.

We all had fun in the van, Leilah and my family, telling jokes and swapping stories during the long hours on the road. We appreciated her knowledge of the Bible, and she our familiarity with Arab culture. We also enjoyed comparing words from Hebrew and Arabic, both Semitic languages. Arabic words sounded Hebrew to us, while Hebrew often sounded like Arabic to her. We used to compare common roots of similar words, like "egg" (*beid* in Arabic and *beitsa* in Hebrew) and "five" (*hamesh* in Hebrew and *khamsa* in Arabic). And, of course, *shalom* and *salaam* — "peace."

When it was time to part, we promised each other we'd stay in touch and visit each other. I invited her to come to America, but knew that invitations made during travels are rarely taken up.

When we'd returned to Israel we told some friends about Leilah and our families' flour mills.

"The mill at Beit-Tsafafa?" exclaimed one. "I know the mill. And I know how it was destroyed." All eyes turned to him.

"The mill at Beit-Tsafafa was a thorn in our side. It was the tallest building in the village and used as a lookout and a base for sniper attacks on the neighboring Jewish community. Many people were being killed. I was made commander of a small group assigned to get rid of it. I remember as if it were yesterday. It was a cold and rainy night. Our clothes were soaked and our shoes covered with mud. We approached the mill by crawling in the dark. I had some trouble disentangling the wires of the explosives and getting them set up, but finally I succeeded. We left quickly and got back to Jerusalem before dawn. From a distance we heard the explosion and saw the horizon light up. I felt a pang in my chest. We had just blown up an enemy depot that was also a flour mill — a source of bread. But we had no choice.

"When we finally reached home, I realized that my wedding ring was gone. I must have lost it when I was handling the explosives. I felt terrible. It was like a bad omen. I'm not superstitious, but in war you believe all kinds of things. I didn't tell my wife, because I was afraid she'd see it as a bad omen too. When I was cleaning my boots the next morning, I found the ring embedded in the mud stuck to the bottom of the heel.

"Anyway, if you ever see Leilah again, tell her that I didn't really want to blow up the mill."

We did see Leilah again, when she came to America on a visit, and we passed along our friend's message.

26

The View from Mount Nebo

ON OUR LAST DAY IN JORDAN we drove to the top of Mount Nebo. Passing through the fertile fields of Medaba, we reached the narrow road that led some 2500 feet above sea level to the top. Mount Nebo is an uninhabited barren hill covered with gray stones and scattered thorny bushes. Looking westward toward Israel, I could see the Jordan River and the Judean hills rising beyond. How astonishing a view! I used to look at the mountains of Moab from Israel, never imagining that one day I would be looking from the other direction.

Mount Nebo has always been shrouded in mystery. More than three thousand years ago Moses stood here gazing at the Jordan River and beyond, preparing to bring the Israelites to Canaan. After liberating his people from bondage in Egypt and wandering in the desert for forty years, after giving them the Ten Commandments and a set of laws to govern their lives, he had finally reached the threshold of the promised land. In spite of his one hundred twenty years, the Bible says, "his eye was not dim, nor his vigor abated." But Moses never crossed the river. He met his death on Mount Nebo.

And the Lord spoke to Moses . . . , "Get up this mountain, Mount Nebo, . . . and behold the land of Canaan
which I give to the children of Israel. And die on the
mountain where you go up and be gathered unto thy
people. . . . thou shalt see the land before thee but thou
shalt not get there."

Legend has it that Moses beseeched God to turn him
into a bird, so he could fly to Canaan, or a fish, so he could
swim there, or the dust of the earth, so he could be blown
across. "Why should I die?" Years ago, an anonymous poet
had Moses pose that question to God, and gave the reply:
"And God answers: 'Lest it be said, "He spoke to God face
to face/And then the skin of his face shone/And he has become like God."'"

An ancient story recounts that God kept Moses' tomb
hidden because He feared that the people of Israel might
cry so loudly and heart-rendingly before it that He might
succumb to their appeal and bring Moses back to life. So
He made his servant's sepulchre inaccessible forever. When
the people stood on the mountain they saw it in the valley.
When they stood in the valley they saw it on the mountain.

According to the Bible, Moses' death was God's punishment for a single act of hastiness and arrogance. When
the Israelites were wandering in the desert, desperate for
water, God instructed Moses to take his rod, to gather the
people, and to speak to the rock, so that it would yield water. But Moses lifted his hand and with his rod smote the
rock twice and fresh water came gushing out. "And the Lord
spoke to Moses . . . , 'Because you believed me not . . . you

shall not bring the congregation into the land which I had promised you'"

Some read the tale of Moses' death as a story of change. Moses, the spiritual leader, had to pass the reins to Joshua, a military man, because the new task of crossing the Jordan and conquering the land of Canaan called for a different kind of leadership. Moses needed to relinquish power to a lesser man, perhaps, but to one better equipped for the new challenge. Others read the story as a metaphor for the mortality of all humans, for the tragedy of incompleteness. During the early Zionist pioneering era, a poet known simply as Rachel sang of the Nebo in every one of us:

> Stretching our arms, gazing afar off,
> Not a person to be seen,
> Only each with his own Nebo
> In that wide expanse.

Nebo is the unfinished dream of nations, too, the recognition that other nations pursue quests different from our own and that we all have to give up our optimal aspirations and accomodate to the reality of sharing the land with others.

Israel has come a long way since my father's time. From an economic perspective, its GNP is twice that of Egypt, Syria, and Jordan combined. By 1995 it had established political ties with 155 nations, compared to only 75 countries twenty years ago. Immigrants of diverse ethnic backgrounds were integrated fairly successfully. Achievements in the cultural sphere have been spectacular. Thousands of books are being published every year; fine symphony orchestras play for thousands of avid listeners; several major universities serve a large body of students pursuing science and the humanities; new poets and writers are continually emerging; cultural centers are being built and archeological sites unearthed. One of the most notable achievements has been the revival of the Hebrew language from a dormant tongue used only in prayer and liturgy to a rich, living language — a renaissance rarely matched in history. These are formidable accomplishments. But the attainment of a comprehensive and lasting peace with its Arab neighbors has unfortunately eluded Israel.

The Arab nations have also made significant strides during the same period. They achieved independence from two successive empires, the Ottoman and the British. Their standard of living has improved, and they are the providers of a significant portion of energy for the industrialized countries. Islam is now the fastest-growing religion in the world. But despite these achievements they are facing overpopulation, totalitarian regimes, internal strife, and the threat of fundamentalism, and peace still eludes them.

Of course there has been much progress. When Yitzhak Rabin was Israel's ambassador to the United States, he was once asked, "Are discussions going on between you and the Arabs?" His response was, "They don't recognize our existence. How can you expect them to negotiate with those who do not exist?" Today, there are peace agreements with Egypt and Jordan and the beginnings of a process with the Palestinians.

Yitzhak Rabin was a man of considerable military talent, indomitable courage, and far-reaching vision. He brought the people to the top of the mountain and, like Moses, he died before his mission was accomplished. King Abdullah, a charismatic leader and a man of great aspirations for his country and for all Arabs, was also cut down with only part of his dream in his hand

I know that my father visited Mount Nebo more than fifty years ago, but I can only guess at his thoughts as he stood there. Having delved into his memoirs and visited the royal palace in Amman and the sites mentioned in my father's story, I think I have gained a new perspective on my father's experiences in Jordan and his friendship with its king. I used to think of that friendship as an oddity, a matter of opportunity and luck — exciting and exotic but of no particular consequence in the larger scheme of things. I see it differently now. I believe that my father's life in Amman was a microcosm of events in the world around him.

The meeting between my father and King Abdullah might have been coincidental, but the relationship that evolved between them was not. The two men were born within a few years of each other, one in Mecca and the other in Jerusalem, the cradles of great religions. Their identities were rooted in those cities. They learned how to read from the Koran and the Bible, and they used them as guides. These books inspired them to reach past the immediate and the mundane, and to seek connections between the traditions of the past and the possibilities of the future.

I think they had a great deal in common. Both abhorred the tyranny of routine, of rules arbitrarily imposed (especially those set by the British), and they appreciated the dramatic, outlandish, playful, and ridiculous. Both were poets at heart. Through verse and word, Abdullah sang his praise of noble horses, the vastness of the desert, and his profound devotion to Allah, while my father expressed his adoration of the world by creating objects of almost infinite shade and pattern

Both men were given to grand gestures. Perhaps this is why neither man could hold on to money. King Abdullah suffered from chronic debt because of his gallant generosity and his appetite for great and beautiful things he could not afford. Despite the volume of his work, my father never made money because he charged very little. He was far more interested in his projects and the people he worked for than in making money. He spent whatever profits he made during the Amman period on a new factory built of stone in northern Jerusalem. The bathrooms were lined with marble and the workers' dining room decorated with a mosaic mural depicting themes of work and nature. The factory also contained an olive-wood-paneled library, containing books and magazines devoted to various crafts, which my father had collected over the years, as well as a number of notebooks that my father had filled with words he had found in the Bible to describe modern tools and building techniques. Passersby used to mistake the factory for a bank. But unlike a bank, it had nothing to do with the business of making money. On the contrary, it ate up all reserves.

I remember my father describing the hospitality so deeply rooted in Bedouin tradition. Guests were asked no questions and treated with great care, even if they were sworn enemies. A mortal enemy would be permitted three days of grace once he was outside the boundaries of the tent. My father used to wonder aloud about his own proverbial three days of grace, and when they would come to an end.

Instead the bonds between host and guest grew stronger. My father came to recognize the king's quick intelligence, humor, and sense of beauty, as well as his longing and sadness. And the king came to appreciate my father's straightforwardness, honesty, pride, and humility.

Along with other Israelis of European origin, my father was enamored of Arab culture. Looking for their roots in the ancient new land, Jews in Palestine turned to the Bible as a way of reviving Hebrew. They embraced archeology as a national pastime, searching for the secret of their origins and their connection to the land. And they often turned to the Arab culture as an alternative to the lifestyle of the European shtetl, which they were eager to shed. They enriched their cuisine with Arab spices, decorated their homes with brass and inlaid mother of pearl, added an Arab trill to their music, and cursed in rich Arabic idioms. My father so relished the Arabic language, and all of its proverbs and metaphors, that he incorporated it into his Hebrew. I remember his distress with modern Israeli architects who built multilevel dwellings on top of Jerusalem's hills, defying the natural contours and ignoring the flowing lines of the land. He used to contrast these structures with Arab dwellings, which he felt were constructed in partnership with nature, not against it — close to the ground and hugging the slopes of the hills.

The alienation of Arabs from Jews and Jews from Arabs was anathema to him. He had grown up playing with Arabs in Jerusalem, speaking their language, becoming versed in their habits and comfortable with their traditions. That was why he was so taken with a man, a king, who embodied so much of what he had grown up admiring.

Yet my father and King Abdullah held basic beliefs that were inherently antagonistic. They were born when Arab nationalism and Jewish Zionism were dawning, and they grew into adulthood when those movements gained momentum and headed toward collision. The collision came, with Abdullah as chief commander of all Arab forces, and Mendel Cohen a soldier in the Israeli Defense Force.

Despite the war and a prolonged state of belligerency, Israel's hopes for a peaceful settlement had always centered on Abdullah. Of all the Arab leaders he was the most accessible, the most willing to consider a compromise that might lead to coexistence. The undercurrents of a peace process were always there, although the peace itself never surfaced during his lifetime.

I see my father's experiences in Jordan as having contributed to that undercurrent, though I do not believe that his loyalty to King Abdullah had an explicitly political purpose. It wasn't until the outbreak of the war in 1948 that I even heard him mention the politics of peace and war with Jordan. For all his Zionist fervor, he abhorred political parties, bureaucracy, and slogans. He never exploited his Amman experience for personal power or status, nor offered his services as an emissary between the king and Israel. He did his part by living there in peace, devising plans for homes and palaces, building medical clinics and hospitals, and quietly gaining the respect of Abdullah and his court.

My father lived by the belief that peace cannot survive by grand proclamations and governmental agreements alone. It gains life in the daily commerce among people, when it is celebrated in the streets and sung by mothers who can tuck their children into bed at night without dread.

Observers of life's designs find patterns within patterns. The vein of a leaf reflects the shape of the branch on which it hangs, which reflects the shape of larger branches, and so forth. Scientists look for design where there seems none: the jagged outline of a beach, a river's erratic course, the seemingly random behavior of earthquakes and economies. All reveal patterns when viewed from a different scale of time or place. "Self-similarity" the scientists call it — or, as the poet William Blake put it, "the world in a grain of sand." My father's personal experience in Jordan, inconsequential as it may appear, may have been one grain containing the pattern of larger scheme.

When my father climbed Mount Nebo fifty years ago he wouldn't have foreseen that one day an Israeli prime minister would be killed by one of his own countrymen. But he would have been no stranger to the thought that peace might reign between the peoples of Israel and Jordan, for his friendship with Abdullah had provided a pattern. And I feel sure that he, ever the optimist, would have recited the Sim Shalom, the prayer for peace.

> Grant us peace, Your most precious gift, O eternal source of peace.
> Give us the will to proclaim its message to all the peoples of the earth . . .
> Strengthen the bonds of friendship among the inhabitants of all lands.
> And may the love of Your name hallow every home and every heart.
> We praise you, O God, the Source of Peace.

SUGGESTED READING

Abdullah, King of Jordan. *Memoirs*. London: Jonathan Cape, 1950. An autobiography describing King Abdullah's early life in the Hejaz, the period of exile in Turkey, the Arab Revolt during the First World War, and the establishment of the Hashemite monarchy in Jordan.

Cohen, Mendel. *At the Court of King Abdullah* (in Hebrew). Tel Aviv: Am-Oved, 1981. The experiences of Mendel Cohen, a Jewish builder-carpenter at the court of King Abdullah, and the friendship that evolved between them.

Collins, Larry and Dominique Lapierre. *O Jerusalem!* New York: Simon and Schuster, 1972. The struggle over Jerusalem during the war of 1948.

Fromkin, David. *A Peace to End All Peace*. New York: Avon Books, 1989. The fall of the Ottoman Empire and the rise of new forces in the Middle East.

Glubb, Sir John Bagot. *The Story of the Arab Legion*. London: Hodder and Stoughton, 1948. A firsthand report by the British brigadier who ran the Arab Legion and befriended the Bedouin of Transjordan. Reprinted by Da Capo Press, New York, 1976.

Hussein, King of Jordan. *Uneasy Lies the Head*. New York: Bernard Geis Associates, 1962. An autobiography which covers the assassination of King Abdullah, the formative years of Hussein's rule, and his political struggles.

Kirkbride, Sir Alec Seath. *A Crackle of Thorns*. London: John Murray, 1956. *From the Wings: Amman Memoirs*. London: Frank Cass, 1976. The memoirs of a British Resident and ambassador who lived in Jordan for many years and formed close ties with King Abdullah.

Lawrence, T. E. *Seven Pillars of Wisdom*. New York: Doubleday, 1935; various reprints. A firsthand account by the man better known as Lawrence of Arabia, of the Arab Revolt against Turkey in 1916 and the British conquests in the Middle East during the First World War.

Meir, Golda. *My Life*. New York: Putnam, 1975. An autobiography covering Meir's early immersion in the Zionist movement, immigration to Palestine, and political career, including the details of Meir's meetings with King Abdullah prior to the outbreak of the war of 1948.

Miller, Judith. *God Has Ninety-Nine Names*. New York: Simon and Schuster, 1996. A detailed, firsthand report of the rise of Muslim militancy in the Middle East, including Jordan and Israel.

Morris, James, *The Hashemite Kings*. New York: Pantheon Books, 1959. A history of the Hashemite kings — Hussein and Ali in the Hejaz; Abdullah, Talal, and Hussein in Jordan; and Faisal, Ghazi, and Faisal in Iraq.

Satloff, Robert B. *From Abdullah to Hussein: Jordan in Transition*. New York: Oxford University Press, 1994. An analysis of the political struggle in Jordan between the end of Abdullah's reign and the accession of King Hussein.

Shlaim, Avi. *Collusion Across the Jordan*. New York: Columbia University Press, 1988. A comprehensive discussion of the relations between King Abdullah and the Jewish community in Palestine from 1921 through the war of 1948, the peace negotiations that followed, and Abdullah's assassination in 1951.

Wilson, Mary C. *King Abdullah, Britain, and the Making of Jordan*. New York: Cambridge University Press, 1987. A biography of King Abdullah, with special emphasis on his relations with the British and the Palestinians.